AURANGZEB

*The Life and Legacy of India's
Most Controversial King*

AUDREY TRUSCHKE

Stanford University Press
STANFORD, CALIFORNIA

Stanford University Press
Stanford, California

©2017 by the Board of Trustees of the Leland Stanford Junior University.
All rights reserved.

Printed in the United States of America on acid-free, archival-quality paper

Library of Congress Cataloging-in-Publication Data

Names: Truschke, Audrey, author.
Title: Aurangzeb : the life and legacy of India's most controversial king /
    Audrey Truschke.
Description: Stanford, California : Stanford University Press, 2017. |
    Includes bibliographical references and index.
Identifiers: LCCN 2016049916 (print) | LCCN 2016050556 (ebook) |
    ISBN 9781503602038 (cloth : alk. paper) | ISBN 9781503602571 (pbk. : alk.
    paper) | ISBN 9781503602595 (ebook) | ISBN 9781503602595 (e-book)
Subjects: LCSH: Aurangzeb, Emperor of Hindustan, 1618-1707. | Aurangzeb,
    Emperor of Hindustan, 1618-1707—Relations with Hindus. | Mogul
    Empire—Kings and rulers—Biography.
Classification: LCC DS461.7 .T78 2016 (print) | LCC DS461.7 (ebook) |
    DDC 954.02/58092 [B] —dc23
LC record available at https://lccn.loc.gov/2016049916

Designed by Bruce Lundquist

Typeset at Stanford University Press in 10/15 Adobe Caslon

For mom

Contents

Illustrations

Preface and Acknowledgments

This book began with a Twitter message asking if I wanted to write an accessible biography of one of the Mughal kings. The discussion quickly migrated to email, and I settled on Aurangzeb Alamgir as the subject. That this book was first formulated via social media is appropriate because the Aurangzeb fever that has gripped modern India often surfaces most virulently on platforms such as Twitter and Facebook. In this short biography I address Aurangzeb's vibrant, ongoing presence in popular culture. From a historian's point of view, however, Aurangzeb is first and foremost a Mughal king about whom most people know lamentably little. This book is an attempt to introduce the historical Aurangzeb— in all of his complexity—to a wide readership.

For the sake of narrative flow and ease of reading, the text is presented without footnotes. It is already difficult to get at Aurangzeb's life and ruling strategies, and footnotes would have posed yet another obstacle. Readers who want to know my sources will find the information in the Bibliographical Essay and the Notes. The Postscript will interest those who desire to learn more about how historians think about the past and analyze premodern sources.

.   .   .

I owe many debts of gratitude in writing this short book. For sharing unpublished work on Aurangzeb, I thank Allison Busch, Munis Faruqui, Supriya Gandhi, Anne Murphy, Heidi

Pauwels, Yael Rice, Samira Sheikh, and Cynthia Talbot. I also thank Yael Rice for her help with images in the book, especially for discovering the Mead Art Museum painting of Aurangzeb, and I look forward to her future work on this image. I thank the following for feedback, comments, and assistance at various stages of this project: Qamar Adamjee, Purnima Dhavan, Wendy Doniger, Richard Eaton, Munis Faruqui, Thomas Blom Hansen, Santhi Kavuri-Bauer, Azfar Moin, Sheldon Pollock, Simran Jeet Singh, Anand Taneja, Taymiya Zaman, and the Stanford Mellon Postdoctoral Fellowship. All opinions, arguments, and errors in this book are mine alone.

Writing about Aurangzeb, one of the most hated men in Indian history, is no light decision, and I owe a special acknowledgment in this regard. My heartfelt gratitude to those who advised me to write the book when I wavered about whether to do so—you know who you are, and I am much obliged.

Note on Scholarly Conventions

Readers will find the following text free of footnotes and dia-
critics. I detail my sources in the Bibliographical Essay and the
Notes. I give non-English words and names in their most common Romanized form and generally omit special characters.

Time Line of Select Events from Aurangzeb's Life and Reign

1618   Aurangzeb is born

1633   Aurangzeb faces a mad elephant

1634   Aurangzeb celebrates his coming of age ceremony

1637   Aurangzeb's first wedding

1653–54   Aurangzeb's romance with the musician Hirabai

1657   Dilras Banu Begum, Aurangzeb's wife, dies

1657   Shah Jahan falls ill, and the war of succession begins

1658   Aurangzeb's first coronation ceremony

1659   Aurangzeb's second coronation ceremony

1659   Dara Shukoh executed

1661   Murad Bakhsh executed

1663   Raja Raghunatha dies

1666   Shah Jahan dies

1666   Shivaji flees from the Mughal court

1667   *Fatawa-i Alamgiri* begun

1669   Public darshans of the emperor discontinued

1669   Benares's Vishvanatha Temple destroyed

1673–74   Construction completed on Badshahi Masjid in
            Lahore

1675   Tegh Bahadur executed

1679–80   Rathor-Sisodia Rebellion

1679   Reinstatement of the jizya tax

1679   Hindu representation in Mughal nobility begins
            to rise

1680   Shivaji dies
1681   Prince Akbar rebels
1681   Aurangzeb moves to the Deccan
1685–86   Siege of Bijapur
1687   Fall of Golconda
1689   Sambhaji executed
1698   Fall of Jinji (Gingee)
1704   Prince Akbar dies in exile
1704   Jizya tax remitted for Deccan
1705   Amar Singh dedicates Persian *Ramayana* to
            Aurangzeb
1707   Aurangzeb dies

AURANGZEB

CHAPTER I

Introducing Aurangzeb

Unforgettable Aurangzeb

I came as a stranger, and I leave as a stranger.

—*Aurangzeb, letter written on the verge of death*

When the Mughal emperor Aurangzeb looked back at his life in 1707 at the ripe age of eighty-eight, he saw failure.

From his deathbed Aurangzeb penned several poignant letters to his sons voicing his gravest fears, including that God would punish his impiety. But, most of all, he lamented his flaws as a king. To his youngest son, Kam Bakhsh, he expressed anxiety that his officers and army would be ill-treated after his death. To his third son, Azam Shah, he admitted deeper doubts: "I entirely lacked in rulership and protecting the people. My precious life has passed in vain. God is here, but my dimmed eyes do not see his splendor."

Aurangzeb ruled for forty-nine years over a population of 150 million people. He expanded the Mughal Empire to its greatest extent, subsuming most of the Indian subcontinent under a single imperial power for the first time in human history. He made lasting contributions to the interpretation and exercise of legal codes and was renowned—by people of all backgrounds and religious stripes—for his justice. He was quite possibly the richest man of his day and boasted a treasury overflowing with gems, pearls, and gold, including the spectacular Kohinoor diamond. But these accomplishments

failed to assuage his angst about his political deficiencies in
his final days.

To both Azam Shah and Kam Bakhsh, Aurangzeb also
confessed his religious shortcomings and the bitter divine judgment he believed he would soon face. A devout Muslim, he
thought that he had "chosen isolation from God" both in this
life and the next. And while he came into the world unbur-
dened, he flinched at the idea of entering the afterlife saddled
with the weight of his sins. He ended his final letter to Azam
with an evocative, lingering flourish, pronouncing his farewell
thrice, "Goodbye, goodbye, goodbye."

.   .   .

Aurangzeb exited this world more than three hundred years ago,
in the winter of 1707. He was buried in a simple, open-air grave
in Khuldabad, Maharashtra. In contrast to Humayun's imposing
tomb of red sandstone in Delhi or Shah Jahan's lavish resting
place at the magnificent Taj Mahal in Agra, Aurangzeb's grave
made no demand that he be remembered. In accordance with
Aurangzeb's wishes, the tomb was plain and unmarked, located
within a Sufi shrine. Over the centuries, marble floors were
added, as well as a marble railing and an identifying plaque.
Even with these embellishments, however, the modesty of
Aurangzeb's tomb issues a strong contrast to the massive blocks
of stone that boldly proclaim the burial sites and earthly legacies
of his predecessors.

Aurangzeb may have been content to be forgotten, but the
world is not ready to let him go. Aurangzeb lives on as a vibrant
figure in public memory in twenty-first-century India and
Pakistan. In India people hotly debate his reign and often condemn him as a vile oppressor of Hindus. Whereas Aurangzeb
questioned his legacy, many Indians today have no doubt that

he was a zealous bigot who ruled by the sword and left behind a trail of Hindu tears. Recent political attempts to erase
Aurangzeb from the face of modern India—such as by renaming Aurangzeb Road in Delhi—have injected new life into
debates about this emperor and India's Islamic past. In nearby
Pakistan Aurangzeb fares only slightly better. Some follow the
Indian line that Aurangzeb was a straight-up bigot, whereas
others view him as one of the few truly righteous Muslim rulers
of old. Precious little history surfaces in these modern visions.

Rather, as misinformation and condemnations of Aurangzeb
swirl about twenty-first-century South Asia, the man himself
remains an enigma.

.   .   .

Aurangzeb was the sixth ruler of the Mughal Empire, a polity
of vast proportions. Although the world outside of the subcontinent rarely recalls the Mughals today, in their time they were a
subject of intense fascination and awe. By 1600, the population
of the Mughal kingdom outstripped the entirety of Europe, and
Mughal wealth was unmatched in the world. Aurangzeb rose
to power in 1658 in the midst of a bloody war of succession that
left two of his brothers dead, a third exiled to Burma, and his
father imprisoned. Aurangzeb named himself the "Seizer of the
World" (Alamgir) and lived up to the title by seizing kingdom
after kingdom during his forty-nine-year reign.

Even during his lifetime, Aurangzeb captured imaginations
across the world. In 1675 John Dryden, then poet laureate of
England, penned *Aureng-zebe*, a heroic tragedy about the reigning Mughal sovereign. Meanwhile, European travelers traversed
India in increasing numbers, and many sought an audience with
the famed Aurangzeb Alamgir. British, Dutch, Portuguese, and
French traders established operations in pockets of the subcon-

tinent and pursued trade agreements with the Mughals. From a Mughal perspective, however, Europeans were small fish. Aurangzeb, like his predecessors, was preoccupied with ruling one of the largest empires in world history, a kingdom encompassing 3.2 million square kilometers (roughly the size of mod-

The Mughal Empire in 1707. Reproduced with permission from Juggernaut Books.

ern India) and esteemed for its riches, prosperity, and religious and cultural diversity.

Unlike other Mughal rulers, who have attracted significant attention from historians, Aurangzeb has been neglected over the past several decades. The task of capturing the life of this king, about whom we know surprisingly little, is far from straightforward. Aurangzeb was a complex emperor whose life was shaped by an assortment of sometimes conflicting desires and motivations, including power, justice, piety, and the burden of Mughal kingship. Such a man would be a challenging historical subject under any circumstances but especially so given the gulf of cultural knowledge that stands between his time and our own.

Aurangzeb is also a live wire of history that sparks fires in the present day. Current popular visions of Aurangzeb are more fiction than reality, however. If we can pierce the haze of myth that shrouds Aurangzeb today, we can begin to recover perhaps the single most important political figure of seventeenth-century India. Since no path to the past can begin anywhere but in the present, I turn first to the imagined Aurangzeb of our times. I then analyze the man himself as both a product of his age and an emperor who shaped the times in which he lived.

The Myth of Aurangzeb the Villain

The last of the so-called "Grand Mughals," Aurungzeb, tried to put back the clock, and in this attempt stopped it and broke it up.

—*Jawaharlal Nehru*

The year 2015 was a bad one for Aurangzeb. A debate raged for much of the year over whether to strip the Mughal emperor's name from a major thoroughfare in Delhi. The reason, as given by a local Sikh group that raised the idea, was that Aurangzeb was "one of the most **tyrannical tormentor perpetrator**

of Intolerant Inhuman Barbaric crimes in India" [*sic*]. A few
Members of Parliament affiliated with the Hindu nationalist
Bharatiya Janata Party (BJP) jumped on this bandwagon and issued their own calls to tear what they viewed as a painful page
out of Delhi's history, or at least erase the offending ruler's name
from the city's road signs. In late August of 2015 New Delhi officials capitulated and rechristened the street A.P.J. Abdul Kalam
Road, after India's eleventh president. A week later, city employees crept out in the dead of night and chiseled Aurangzeb's name
off the street signs.

Rather than induce a society-wide amnesia about Aurangzeb,
however, such events only propelled him into the forefront of
people's minds. A mere month later, in October 2015, a Shiv
Sena MP was caught on tape hurling invectives at a civic official, including "Aurangzeb ki aulad" (Aurangzeb's progeny). Such
language mirrors "Babur ki aulad" (Babur's progeny), a term of
abuse lobbed against Indian Muslims, especially during the late
1980s and early 1990s in the lead up to the demolition of the
Babri Masjid in Ayodhya by a right-wing, Hindutva mob. But
why replace Babur with Aurangzeb?

·   ·   ·

From a divisive Hindu nationalist perspective, Babur and
Aurangzeb are to some degree interchangeable as oppressive
Muslim conquerors. In this sense Aurangzeb stands in for an
entire category of "orthodox Muslims" who are supposedly implicated in unsavory aspects of India's past and, consequently,
unwelcome in India's present. It is not incidental that Aurangzeb is widely believed to have been the most pious of the Mughal kings. Aurangzeb thus typifies zealous Muslims overall—
both past and present—who allegedly threaten Indian society
by virtue of their religiosity. In this formulation Indian and

Hindu cultures are collapsed into a single, flattened entity that offers little breathing room for other religious groups.

But Aurangzeb also holds a special, uncoveted place among India's reviled kings. Common opinion, even among those who do not share the sentiments of the BJP and like-minded Hindu nationalist groups, pillories Aurangzeb as a callous Islamist oppressor who despised everything about India, especially Hindus. Across the border in Pakistan, too, many endorse the vision of an evil Aurangzeb, even responsible for South Asia's modern woes. As Shahid Nadeem, a Pakistani playwright, recently put it: "Seeds of Partition were sown when Aurangzeb triumphed over [his brother] Dara Shikoh." Such far-fetched suggestions would be farcical, if so many did not endorse them.

The Pakistani playwright's view has a precedent in the writing of Jawaharlal Nehru, a founding father of modern India who was no fan of Aurangzeb. In his *Discovery of India*, first published in 1946, Nehru listed Aurangzeb's purported faults at length, rebuking him as "a bigot and an austere puritan." He excoriated the sixth Mughal king as a dangerous throwback who "put back the clock" and ended up destroying the Mughal Empire. Perhaps Nehru's most damning blow was to pronounce Aurangzeb too Muslim to be a successful Indian king: "When Aurungzeb began to oppose [the syncretism of earlier Mughal rulers] and suppress it and to function more as a Moslem than an Indian ruler, the Mughal Empire began to break up." For Nehru, Aurangzeb's adherence to Islam crippled his ability to rule India.

Nehru was hardly original in his censure of Aurangzeb as dangerously pious and therefore a bad emperor. Such views were espoused by many of Nehru's contemporaries, including Jadunath Sarkar, the foremost twentieth-century historian of Aurangzeb.

British colonial thinkers had long impugned the Mughals on a range of charges, including that they were effeminate, oppressive, and Muslims. As early as 1772, Alexander Dow remarked in a discussion of Mughal governance that "the faith of Mahommed is peculiarly calculated for despotism; and it is one of the greatest causes which must fix for ever the duration of that species of government in the East." For the British the solution to such an entrenched problem was clear: British rule over India. While Indian independence leaders rejected this final step of colonial logic, many swallowed the earlier parts wholesale. Such ideas filtered to society at large via textbooks and mass media, and several generations have continued to eat up and regurgitate the colonial take that Aurangzeb was a tyrant driven by religious fanaticism.

.   .   .

Over the centuries, many commentators have spread the myth of the bigoted, evil Aurangzeb on the basis of shockingly thin evidence. Many false ideas still mar popular memory of Aurangzeb, including that he massacred millions of Hindus and destroyed thousands of temples. Neither of these commonly believed "facts" is supported by historical evidence, although some scholars have attempted, usually in bad faith, to provide an alleged basis for such tall tales. More common than bald-faced lies, however, have been biased interpretations of cherry-picked episodes selected with the unabashed goal of supporting a foregone rebuke of Aurangzeb. For instance, detractors trumpet that Aurangzeb destroyed certain temples without acknowledging that he issued many orders protecting Hindu temples and granted stipends and land to Brahmins. They denounce that he restricted the celebration of Holi without mentioning that he also clamped down on Muharram and Eid festivities. They omit altogether that Aurangzeb consulted with Hindu ascetics on health matters and employed more Hindus in his administration than any prior Mughal ruler by a substantial margin. We cannot reconcile these less-frequently reported but historically important aspects of Aurangzeb's rule with the fictitious image of this ruler as propelled by religious-based hate.

Of course, no one would contend that Aurangzeb was without faults. It is not difficult to identify specific actions taken by Aurangzeb that fail to meet modern democratic, egalitarian, and human rights standards. Aurangzeb ruled in a premodern world of kingdoms and empires, and his ideas about violence, state authority, and everything else were conditioned by the time and place in which he lived. Aurangzeb's contemporaries included such kings as Charles II of England, Louis XIV of France, and the Ottoman Sultan Suleiman II. No one asserts that these historical figures were "good rulers" under present-day norms because it makes little sense to assess the past by contemporary criteria. The aim of historical study is something else entirely.

Historians seek to comprehend people on their own terms, as products of particular times and places, and explain their actions and impacts. We need not absolve our subjects of study of guilt, and we certainly do not need to like them. But we strive to hold back judgment long enough so that the myth of Aurangzeb can fade into the background and allow room for a more nuanced and compelling story to be told.

Recovering Aurangzeb the Man

The stability of the foundation of sovereignty depends upon justice (*'adalat*).
—Maxim for rulers, quoted approvingly by Aurangzeb

Aurangzeb organized his life as ruler of Hindustan around a few key ideals and preoccupations. He wanted to be a just king, a good Muslim, and a sustainer of Mughal culture and customs.

Aurangzeb also headed an expansionist state and so labored to extend imperial control over the subcontinent and its inhabitants, often using violence. My narrative of Aurangzeb revolves around his attempts to pursue these core values, above all justice, and includes instances in which he forfeited his ideals in the hunt for raw power.

Aurangzeb's vision of justice was deeply colored by the wider Islamic tradition, much of which had little to do with theology. Premodern "Islamic" ideas about justice drew extensively from Persian and Greek philosophies that predated Islam. In this vision divisive concepts such as *jihad* and *jizya* (holy war and poll tax) were less important than the ideals of *akhlaq* and *adab* (political and ethical conduct). Aurangzeb was also influenced by his imperial predecessors and modeled himself on prior Mughal kings. Of course, Aurangzeb's ideas about justice do not tally with those commonly accepted today. But that is hardly the point. In lieu of judging Aurangzeb by contemporary standards, I seek to construct a historical account of his life and reign and thereby recover the man and the king from underneath the mounds of misinformation that we have blindly accepted for centuries.

Aurangzeb's devotion to justice, piety, and the Mughal state are recurrent subjects in Persian histories, the king's letters, and other primary sources from the seventeenth and eighteenth centuries. Critical readings of these Persian works form the backbone of my narrative of Aurangzeb, along with research in Hindi, Sanskrit, and other languages (for more, see the Bibliographical Essay and Postscript). Aurangzeb's ideas—especially his notions of justice, ethics, and correct Islamic behavior—are often a world apart from how most define these things today. But the question before us is not whether Aurangzeb was a just king. Rather, I want to know what Aurangzeb thought it meant to be a just Mughal king and how that shaped his worldview and actions as emperor of Hindustan.

Understanding Aurangzeb on his own terms is a promising project but one little tried to date. This approach can help us better grasp Aurangzeb's impact on medieval India and his crucial position within Indo-Muslim history. Moreover, grounded historical claims can temper the passions of the present that so often present Aurangzeb as something he never was. That my suggested intervention in current distortions of Aurangzeb is based on serious history is especially germane. In contrast, earlier thinkers have tried to defuse the volatile popular image of Aurangzeb by using two distinct tactics that have both failed because they are defensive.

.   .   .

The first futile approach has been to concede that Aurangzeb was a religious tyrant but to contrast him with "heterodox Muslim" Mughal figures, chiefly Akbar and Dara Shukoh. In comparison to the orthodox Aurangzeb, the argument goes, Akbar and Dara absorbed many Hindu ideas and thus became sufficiently "Indian" to be acceptable rulers of the subcontinent. This line of thought does not reconsider or reevaluate Aurangzeb. Instead, he is maligned for supposedly demolishing the culture of tolerance built by Akbar, the third Mughal ruler and Aurangzeb's great-grandfather, and for snatching the Mughal throne out from under Dara Shukoh, Aurangzeb's elder brother. In the grand arc of history, however, Aurangzeb's sectarianism was purportedly counterbalanced by the syncretic legacy of exemplary Indian Muslims. This thinking is shared even by the likes of V. D. Savarkar, an early ideologue for Hindu nationalism. Following this logic, during the debate over renaming Aurangzeb Road in Delhi, the idea was floated to perhaps retitle the street Dara Shukoh Road.

In reality both Akbar and Dara Shukoh, like Aurangzeb, were more complicated than their popular reputations suggest. By holding up Akbar and Dara to balance Aurangzeb, we fail to learn anything new about any of these men and shackle ourselves to ranking Mughal kings according to their purported Muslimness. In such comparisons we also commit the classic error of assuming that everything in Indian history, especially the Indo-Muslim past, was about religion. Aurangzeb was a Muslim, although not the type of Muslim either his modern detractors or supporters suppose him to have been. Moreover, Aurangzeb cannot be reduced to his faith. To be honest to the past, we need to reclaim a fuller picture of him as a prince and an emperor.

· · ·

Taking a different angle of attack, some have argued that we have judged Aurangzeb too harshly. Perhaps India's most loathed Muslim evildoer was not so heinous after all?

This argument rests on correcting misinterpretations and presenting overlooked aspects of Aurangzeb's reign, which are largely accurate. Contrary to popular belief, for instance, Aurangzeb never oversaw a large-scale conversion program that offered non-Muslims a choice between Islam or the sword. Aurangzeb did not destroy thousands of Hindu temples (a few dozen is a more likely number). He did not perpetrate anything resembling a genocide of Hindus. In fact, Aurangzeb appointed Hindus to top positions in his government. He protected the interests of Hindu religious groups, even ordering fellow Muslims to cease harassing Brahmins. He tried to provide safe roads and basic law and order for all of his subjects.

Setting the record straight falls within a historian's purview, and this much is true: Aurangzeb was less malevolent than his contemporary reputation would have us believe. But by merely trumpeting that Aurangzeb lacked total depravity, we do not move beyond the terms set by popular condemnations of Aurangzeb. More troubling is that we fail to do justice to India's intricate past. Surely there is more to say about a man who ruled for half a century and reshaped the political landscape of precolonial India than whether he is palatable according to twenty-first-century sensibilities? We must resist the strong, modern instinct to summarily judge Aurangzeb and, instead, first recover what we can about the actions and ideas of this influential king.

We need a fresh narrative about Aurangzeb. Here I offer one such story.

· · ·

My narrative incorporates many aspects of Aurangzeb's life and reign little known today and thereby adds much-needed historical depth to a misunderstood king. It also addresses the alleged "worst" of Aurangzeb—his temple desecrations, Machiavellian political instincts, violent tactics, persecutions of select religious communities, and so forth—but it is not defined by such topics. Merely countering the misinformation and dubious claims promulgated by Aurangzeb's detractors would be an empty exercise because it would fail to fulfill a core guideline of history: understanding historical figures *on their own terms*.

A good example of this distinction—thinking defensively versus historically—is Aurangzeb's treatment of Hindus. In popular thought Aurangzeb is imagined to have detested all Hindus and sought to stomp them down at every turn. A responsible historian could retort that Aurangzeb handled Hindus differently depending on the circumstances. Frequent conflicts arose between the Mughal state and specific Hindu communities, sometimes involving sensitive religious issues. But toleration and state protection were equally common experiences for Hindus in Aurangzeb's India. This historical correction, although accurate, shares a false assumption with the charges that it answers: namely, that generalizing about Hindus is a fruitful way to think about Aurangzeb's rule.

In reality Aurangzeb pursued no overarching agenda vis-à-vis Hindus within his state. "Hindus" of the day often did not even label themselves as such and rather prioritized a medley of regional, sectarian, and caste identities (e.g., Rajput, Maratha, Brahmin, Vaishnava). As many scholars have pointed out, the word *Hindu* is Persian, not Sanskrit, and only became commonly used self-referentially during British colonialism. The Mughals, too, emphasized differences between groups of "Hindus." For example, Mahabat Khan, who led Mughal efforts in the Deccan for a short period in the early 1670s, preferred "Rajputs and Hindus" among the Mughal nobility, even while fighting the Marathas (who apparently did not count as "Hindu" in this instance). Instead of assessing Mughal-Hindu relations under Aurangzeb as a block, we are better off—in terms of historical grounding—considering specific groups and actions separately. Accordingly, readers will find here no section on Aurangzeb's treatment of Hindus writ large but rather more precise discussions of Hindu nobles who worked for the Mughal state, Brahmin religious leaders, and armed Maratha opposition.

If we think beyond the restricting, communal terms of our day and instead strive to recover the seventeenth-century Mughal world, a striking picture of Aurangzeb emerges. Aurangzeb was an Indian emperor who strove throughout his life to preserve and expand the Mughal Empire, gain political power, and rule with justice.

. . .

Historians agree on certain basic data about Aurangzeb's life. He was born in the autumn of 1618. He held his first coronation ceremony at the age of thirty-nine in 1658. He moved the entire imperial court to the Deccan in 1681, when he was in his mid-sixties, and subsequently conquered Bijapur, Golconda, and even parts of Tamil Nadu. He died in 1707 at the age of eighty-eight. But everything interesting about Aurangzeb comes out in how we string the facts together. In other words, it is the narrative that matters.

My narrative of Aurangzeb investigates both the breadth and depth of the emperor's life and is arranged partly chrono-logically and partly topically. In tracing Aurangzeb's life from childhood to death, we can grasp the major forces that shaped his ideas about Mughal kingship, ethical conduct, and politics and see how these evolved over time. By delving into select episodes and facets of his years on the throne, we gain a deeper appreciation of the motivations that drove Aurangzeb and the outcomes of his hallmark policies.

I begin with the first four decades of Aurangzeb's life, espe-cially his young adult years as a prince who positioned himself to outmaneuver his brothers in the impending war of succes-sion. Aurangzeb secured the throne after a bloody two-year struggle and immediately began adjusting his inherited ruling culture to suit his own needs, a project that unfolded across his nearly fifty-year reign. Three aspects of Aurangzeb's reign help us better grasp his ruling strategies and vision of justice: the imperial bureaucracy, Aurangzeb's view of himself as a moral leader, and his policies regarding Hindu and Jain temples. These topics encompass some of the most controversial facets of Aurangzeb's reign and bring out little-known features. Above all, these sections add historical depth to a king often crudely

caricatured through a single lens. I next narrate the later years
of Aurangzeb's life, including his final decades spent toiling
in the Deccan and his death. I close with a brief discussion of
Aurangzeb's legacy, including the charge that he bears responsibility for the splintering of the Mughal Empire in the eighteenth century.

Based on detailed research, I propose that we can fruitfully
view Aurangzeb as a prince who was enmeshed in a web of
royal family dynamics that shaped his early years and then as an
Indian king who hungered after territory, political power, and a
particular ideal of justice.

CHAPTER 2

Early Years

The Indian Prince's Childhood

It is hoped that his advent will prove fortunate and auspicious to this
eternal dynasty.

—Jahangir's wish upon the birth of his grandson, Aurangzeb

Aurangzeb was born on November 3, 1618, in Dohad, Gujarat,
during the reign of his grandfather, Jahangir. A few weeks later
Aurangzeb's father, Prince Khurram (later known as Shah
Jahan), hosted a birth celebration during which he showed off
his newborn son and gifted heaping trays of gems and dozens
of elephants to the imperial treasury. Despite such a propitious
beginning, however, Aurangzeb would not find his father's favor
easy to secure.

Aurangzeb was Shah Jahan's third son, preceded by his
brothers Dara Shukoh and Shah Shuja and would be followed a
year later by a fourth son, Murad. The four boys were full brothers, all sons of Mumtaz Mahal, Shah Jahan's favorite wife. Like
his brothers, Aurangzeb received a princely education that covered several intellectual and literary traditions.

As part of his curriculum, Aurangzeb studied Islamic religious texts, including the Quran, hadith (sayings of the Prophet
Muhammad), and religious biographies. He also read Turkish
literature and learned the art of calligraphy. Mughal princely
education emphasized the Persian classics, especially the great
poets and scholars that are still beloved today, such as Sa'di,

Nasiruddin Tusi, and Hafiz. Aurangzeb is rumored to have
been especially fond of Rumi's *Masnavi*. These Persian works
shaped the ethics and values of Mughal princes, especially their
ideas about justice, *adab* and *akhlaq*, and kingship.

Aurangzeb may well have been exposed to Persian translations of Sanskrit texts, such as the Hindu epics *Mahabharata*
and *Ramayana*. These translations were sponsored by Aurangzeb's great-grandfather, Akbar, and we know that Akbar recommended the *Mahabharata* to one of his sons as helpful for
a princely education. Aurangzeb also spoke fluent Hindi from
childhood and came from the fourth generation of the Mughal
family to do so. Aurangzeb was versed in literary registers of
Hindi, likely as part of his formal training, and there are even
original compositions in Braj Bhasha, a literary register of premodern Hindi, attributed to him. Mughal princely curriculum
also involved practical instruction in swords, daggers, muskets,
military strategy, and administrative skills.

·   ·   ·

Beyond education, a Mughal prince's childhood was characterized by brotherly rivalry, and Aurangzeb's upbringing proved
no exception.

From a young age the four sons of Shah Jahan were locked
in competition for the Mughal throne. The Mughals inherited a
Central Asian custom that all male family members had equal
claims to political power. Emperor Akbar had managed to narrow
the list of legitimate contenders to sons (thus cutting out nephews
and male cousins), but birth order was largely irrelevant. In the
absence of primogeniture, Shah Jahan's lustrous Peacock Throne
could one day belong to Aurangzeb, if he could outmaneuver his
sibling contenders. As a child, however, Aurangzeb had few opportunities to distinguish himself in comparison to his brothers.

Shah Jahan openly favored his eldest son. Dara Shukoh's first wedding, for example, outshone all others in Mughal history. At the cost of 3.2 million rupees, more than the Mughals had ever spent on a wedding, the royal family put on a show in 1633 whose dimensions are still impressive today. According to a European observer, Peter Mundy, the awe-inspiring firework display stretched for half a mile across the Agra sky. Illustrations of the wedding festivities survive in a copy of the *Padshahnama*, an official chronicle of Shah Jahan's rule, now tucked away in Windsor Castle in England. The vibrant scenes teem with crowds of imperial musicians, gift bearers, well-wishers, and officials who make up a sea of colorful, bejeweled humanity present in honor of Shah Jahan's preferred son. Aurangzeb, fourteen at the time, reportedly attended these events, although he does not merit even an appearance in the hundreds of figures who fill the *Padshahnama* illustrations of the wedding procession.

. . .

A few months after Dara Shukoh's wedding, Aurangzeb found a rare moment to bask in his father's spotlight. Shah Jahan had called for an elephant fight, a favorite royal pastime. Sudhakar and Surat Sundar (Mughal elephants often had Hindi names) faced off, while the king and his three eldest sons followed on horseback in order to keep within close sight of the action. Suddenly, Sudhakar charged at Aurangzeb in a maddened rage. Aurangzeb speared the elephant's head, which enraged the animal further. Sudhakar then gouged the prince's horse and flung Aurangzeb to the ground. Onlookers tried to intervene, Shuja and Raja Jai Singh (Aurangzeb's brother and a prominent Rajput, respectively) with weapons and guards with distracting fireworks. But ultimately only Surat Sundar was able to draw Sudhakar away from Aurangzeb and back into the fight.

Notably, Dara Shukoh was nowhere to be seen during this life-threatening encounter. Written records of the event do not mention his role at all, and in the surviving illustration Dara lurks in the background, safe from both harm and glory.

Abu Talib Kalim, Shah Jahan's poet laureate, penned verses of Persian poetry to memorialize Aurangzeb's bravery. He marveled at how Aurangzeb's spear flashed like lightning and lit up Sudhakar's head. Then, "Out of the gouge inflicted by the prince's spear / gushed the elephant's mind-poisoning madness." Shah Jahan commended Aurangzeb's courage and, for a moment, perhaps even saw his son in his own image. Shah Jahan's court chronicler agreed and paralleled Aurangzeb's fearless feat with Shah Jahan's famous repelling of a raging lion in 1610 while his father, Jahangir, watched.

.   .   .

A few years later Shah Jahan sent Aurangzeb, then only sixteen years old, away from court to help run the empire. For twenty-two long years, between 1635 and 1657, Aurangzeb shuttled across the reaches of the Mughal kingdom, fighting wars in Balkh, Bundelkhand, and Qandahar and administering Gujarat, Multan, and the Deccan.

The prince also carved out time to enjoy himself during these years, such as his whirlwind romance with Hirabai Zainabadi. In 1653 Aurangzeb visited his maternal aunt's house in Burhanpur and fell head over heels in love when he saw Hirabai, a singer and a dancer, playfully pluck a mango from a tree. The two became lovers. Aurangzeb was rumored to have been so taken with the young woman that he even agreed to break his lifelong commitment to temperance and drink wine at her request (she stopped him before the first drop passed his lips). Alas, Hirabai died less than a year later and was buried in Aurangabad. Despite such moments of respite, Aurangzeb spent most of his adult princely years engaged in state business.

Aurangzeb's absence from the royal household did not make his father's heart grow fonder. The prince returned to court rarely during this twenty-two-year period, making only short appearances for compulsory events such as his first marriage in 1637. Aurangzeb proved adept at both administration and military expansion but was often frustrated by decisions from Delhi that seemed designed to undermine his success. In the 1650s, for example, Aurangzeb was forced to withdraw from a few near victories in the Deccan in response to orders from Shah Jahan, acting on the urging of Dara Shukoh.

While Aurangzeb spent his twenties and thirties proving himself on the battlefield, developing administrative abilities, and gaining a formidable reputation, Dara Shukoh leisured at court. Shah Jahan's eldest son was known for his philosophical interests and passed his days in erudite conversations with Hindu and Muslim ascetics. On paper Dara was always ahead of Aurangzeb. The elder brother held the higher rank in the Mughal *mansab* system, which encompassed all state officers, and he was widely understood as Shah Jahan's choice to ascend the throne. But Dara lacked real-world experience beyond the rigidly controlled environment of the central court, which would prove a fatal liability.

Popular memory of Dara Shukoh often extols him as the big "What If" of Indian history. What if "liberal" Dara had become the sixth Mughal king instead of "zealous" Aurangzeb? Would history have turned out differently? Some, inspired by Shahid Nadeem's play *Dara*, have even recently asked: Could King Dara have preemptively averted India's brutal partition in 1947? Misplaced nostalgia aside, the reality is that Dara Shukoh was ill-prepared to either win or rule the Mughal kingdom. In the inevitable showdown between the four brothers for the crown of Hindustan, Dara's favor with an ailing king could not counter Aurangzeb's alliances, tactical skills, and the political acumen he had gained during his decades of traversing the Mughal Empire.

Aurangzeb Seized the World

Ya takht ya tabut (Either the throne or the grave)

—A mantra of Mughal kingship

One morning in September of 1657, Shah Jahan awoke gravely ill and failed to make his daily morning appearance before his subjects at his palatial balcony. He also cancelled court that day. Shah Jahan did not appear in public again for more than a week, and by then the damage had been done. News of the king's debilitation spread like wildfire throughout the kingdom. Shopkeepers panicked, and looting spiked. Shah Jahan's four sons believed their father was on the brink of death, so they seized the opportunity created by this power vacuum to determine—according to time-honored Mughal practices of force and trickery—who would be crowned the next emperor of Hindustan.

Nearly two years passed before the dust of conflict settled and Aurangzeb emerged as the undisputed victor. To ascend the Mughal throne, Aurangzeb outmaneuvered his three brothers—Dara Shukoh, Shah Shuja, and Murad—and his father, Shah Jahan. By the time he finished dealing with his immediate family in the early 1660s, Aurangzeb had executed two of his brothers, driven the third out of India, and locked away his recovered father in Agra's Red Fort. Aurangzeb alone escaped the violence unscathed to rule over an undivided Mughal kingdom.

European travelers were horrified by the brutal, bloody succession battle that engulfed the Mughal royal family. Gemelli

Careri, an Italian who visited Mughal India decades later, lambasted the familial strife as "the unnatural war." John Ovington, an East India Company chaplain in Surat later in Aurangzeb's reign, condemned "such barbarous sacrifices" and summed up the affair as "inhumane." Other European travel writers, such as Francois Bernier and Niccoli Manucci, wrote with gruesome fascination about the stratagems and intrigues of these events, as well as the "lust of domination" that fueled the four brothers, especially Aurangzeb. Indian observers were equally riveted by the details of the struggle, but they were less surprised by its occurrence and, at least at first, by its ruthlessness.

Mughal kingship had long been guided by the blunt Persian expression *ya takht ya tabut* (either the throne or the grave). Shah Jahan ordered the murder of two of his brothers, Khusrau in 1622 and Shahriyar in 1628, and, for good measure, also executed two nephews and two male cousins upon seizing the throne in 1628. Circumstantial evidence suggests that Shah Jahan's father, Jahangir, bore responsibility for the death of Danyal, Jahangir's youngest brother (the ostensible cause was alcohol poisoning). Even the early days of Mughal rule under Babur and Humayun were characterized by violent clashes that pitted brother against brother and son against father.

While Aurangzeb and his brothers expected to fight one another for the throne, neither the timing nor the outcome of the conflict were preordained.

. . .

In 1657 Shah Jahan was sixty-five years old and had already lived longer than any of the four Mughal kings who preceded him. Nonetheless, his illness was sudden and unexpected. Observers at the time lacked consensus on what brought Shah Jahan to death's door. In his characteristically colorful fashion, the Italian

traveler Niccoli Manucci claimed that the libertine ruler overdosed on aphrodisiacs. Manucci's compatriot, Careri, likewise
surmised that Shah Jahan was overcome by "unruly passion"
and had too much sex for an old man. In reality a bladder or
bowel problem was the likely culprit. Regardless of the exact
illness that set off the war of succession, the foundation for conflict between the four princes had been laid years ago.

In the early 1650s, Aurangzeb had forged a secret alliance
with Shah Shuja and Murad to oppose Dara Shukoh. The three
younger brothers knew their father favored his eldest son, and
Dara may have hatched his own plans to murder his brothers
around the same time. As one contemporary Persian account
put it, already in 1652 Dara was "a wolf, thirsty for the blood of
his brothers." Later, when the succession fight was under way,
Aurangzeb allegedly sent a letter to Shah Jahan in which he re-
iterated Dara's murderous intentions, especially his craving for
Aurangzeb's innocent blood. Soon enough, however, Aurangzeb
was the one to commit fratricide.

When Shah Jahan fell ill, Dara Shukoh was the only son
present at court in Delhi. His brothers were each running a
major wing of the empire: Shah Shuja controlled Bengal in the
East, Murad administered Gujarat in the West, and Aurangzeb
was stationed in the Deccan in the South. Dara tried to control
the flow of news to his brothers by detaining informants and
closing roads but to no avail. In addition to hearing about Shah
Jahan's sickness, the three younger brothers also had their ears
filled with rumors about Dara seizing power, ramping up murderous plans for them, and imprisoning their father.

As the fourfold contest crystallized, the nobles of the empire
took sides. Shah Shuja and Murad were formidable opponents,
and both commanded substantial support. But the major com-

petition was between Dara Shukoh and Aurangzeb, and most
Mughal nobles backed one of these two. Royal women were
also involved in Mughal succession struggles, and Shah Jahan's
three daughters chose their favorites to ascend the throne.
Jahanara, the eldest sister, supported Dara Shukoh. Roshanara,
the middle sister, backed Aurangzeb. Gauharara, the youngest,
wagered on Murad. For Aurangzeb, the first step in opposing
Dara was to secure a loose alliance with Murad.

.   .   .

Mistakenly believing his father dead, in December 1657 Murad
declared himself king and held a coronation ceremony in
Gujarat. For Aurangzeb, this preemptive self-crowning was
less threatening than Murad's strong position in one of the
wealthiest provinces of the Mughal Empire and his command
over tens of thousands of troops. In order to coax his youngest brother out of Gujarat, Aurangzeb made a promise that he
likely never intended to keep: Aurangzeb vowed that, upon de-
feating Dara Shukoh and Shah Shuja, he would cede control of
the north and northwest portions of the Mughal kingdom to
Murad. The historian Ishvardas reported that Aurangzeb even
cited to his brother the Persian proverb: "Two hearts united
will cleave a mountain." The ruse worked. Murad marched out
of Gujarat, and his forces, combined with those of Aurangzeb,
overpowered the imperial army in April 1658 at Dharmat, near
Ujjain. The brothers next moved north toward Delhi, seeking
victory in the heart of the Mughal Empire.

   The united troops of Aurangzeb and Murad met Dara Shukoh's fifty-thousand-strong army just east of Agra on a fiercely
hot day in May of 1658. The ensuing clash, known today as the
Battle of Samugarh (fig. 1), proved the decisive moment in de-
termining the Mughal succession crisis. The day prior to the

Figure 1. The Battle of Samugarh. Attributed to Payag, c. 1658. Harvard Art Museums/ Arthur M. Sackler Museum. Gift of Stuart Cary Welch Jr., 1999.298.

confrontation, Aurangzeb rested his and Murad's troops, while Dara's soldiers waited in vain for their foes in the punishing sun, dressed in heavy battle armor. Their strength sapped, many in Dara's army fell as a result of heat alone, with no need of enemy blows to finish them off.

The next day the battle commenced at dawn with both sides well-armed with artillery, cavalry, archers, armored elephants, and infantry. Aurangzeb and Dara Shukoh each sat on an elephant, towering over their respective armies. Their men put up a strong fight, and, in the words of an eighteenth-century historian, "the din of battle rose high in that terror-stricken field." Toward the end of the day Aurangzeb's troops pressed close enough to fire cannons and rockets at the war elephant bearing Dara Shukoh. Fearing for his life, Dara dis-

mounted and fled the battlefield on horseback. He left behind
disarrayed and demoralized troops that were soon routed.

Dara Shukoh escaped to Agra, where Shah Jahan was en-
sconced at the Red Fort, and then absconded to Lahore by way
of Delhi. With their eldest brother on the run, Aurangzeb and
Murad approached the Red Fort at Agra to deal with their recovered father, who remained the nominal head of the Mughal state.

. . .

Shah Jahan tried to meet with Aurangzeb. Citing the Quranic
example of Joseph reuniting with his father, Jacob, after years
apart, the king attempted to cajole his son to agree to an audience. Sensing deceit, Aurangzeb refused. Instead, in early June of
1658 he and Murad besieged the Agra fort with Shah Jahan inside and cut off the water supply. Within days Shah Jahan threw
open the fort's gates and surrendered his treasury, arsenal, and
himself to his two youngest sons. Using his eldest daughter,
Jahanara, as an intermediary, Shah Jahan made a last-ditch effort
to convince Aurangzeb to divide the kingdom five ways with
pieces going to his three brothers plus Aurangzeb's eldest son,
Muhammad Sultan (d. 1676). Many of Shah Jahan's remaining
supporters among the nobility were quicker to accept Aurangzeb's victory and pledged the prince their loyalty before the siege
was even complete.

In the following few weeks tensions surfaced in the alliance
between Aurangzeb and Murad. Murad increased the salaries
of his soldiers and promised quick advancement, enticing some
of Aurangzeb's troops to switch allegiances. Despite his elder
brother's urgings, Murad dragged his feet about pursuing Dara
Shukoh. He even dodged meeting with Aurangzeb. For his part,
Aurangzeb decided that Murad had outlived his usefulness.

Aurangzeb used the pretense of illness to lure his younger

brother to a private meeting in the summer of 1658. After being fed, Murad agreed to rest and so disarmed. Later versions of this tale add that Murad drank wine (while Aurangzeb remained sober) or relaxed under the skilled hands of a masseuse, indulgences that impaired the younger prince's judgment and lulled him into a deep slumber. Once defenseless, Murad was arrested by Aurangzeb's soldiers and thrown in chains. Aurangzeb wasted no time in absorbing his younger brother's army of twenty thousand men.

King of Hindustan

When a celebration is adorned like paradise itself, even the skies rise up from their place to dance.

—Quoted by Khafi Khan, an eighteenth-century historian, to celebrate
Aurangzeb's first coronation

With Murad jailed, Shah Jahan confined, and Dara Shukoh a fugitive, Aurangzeb paused long enough to hold the first of two coronation ceremonies. On July 31, 1658, a date deemed propitious by astrologers, Aurangzeb crowned himself king in Delhi's Shalimar Gardens and adopted the regnal title Alamgir, World Seizer.

Aurangzeb ordered music played and gifts distributed, in accordance with Mughal customs, but he forewent the conventions of striking coins and having the Friday sermon (*khutba*) read in his regnal name. Despite its truncated nature, this moment marked the beginning of Aurangzeb's long reign. An image of this first coronation, painted a few years later, captures both its simplicity and its momentousness. A young Aurangzeb, his beard still black, kneels in the foreground. The emperor's prominent nose and olive-colored skin, features noted by a later visitor to his court, are apparent. He sits erect with no trace

of the bowed shoulders of his later years. Only two other figures witness the moment, a sign of the ceremony's abbreviated
quality. With high hopes for a prosperous, virtuous rule over a
unified Mughal state, the painting depicts a wide shaft of light
breaking through dark storm clouds above and bathing the
newly crowned king in heaven's approval (fig. 2).

.   .   .

After his initial coronation Aurangzeb set off to neutralize his
two footloose brothers: Dara Shukoh and Shah Shuja.

Aurangzeb pursued Dara for months, tracking his older
brother to Lahore, then driving him to Multan and further
south along the Indus River. To avoid being captured, Dara
Shukoh led his dwindling troops over harsh ground, cutting
through jungles and traversing long stretches devoid of fresh
water. He hemorrhaged supporters and eventually ended up in
Gujarat. By the end of September 1658, Aurangzeb left the hunt
for Dara to his loyal officers and turned back toward Delhi to
deal with the approach of Shah Shuja.

Shah Shuja had kept busy throughout the past year. On receiving news of Shah Jahan's ailment in 1657, he had crowned
himself king, complete with the ostentatious title Abul Fauz
(Father of Victory) Nasruddin (Defender of the Faith) Muhammad Timur III Alexander II Shah Shuja Bahadur Ghazi.
But Shah Shuja's dreams of ruling the Mughal kingdom were
short-lived. In February of 1658, before the Battle of Samugarh
(in May of that year) in which Aurangzeb and Murad's combined forces caused Dara Shukoh to flee to Lahore, Shuja
clashed with Dara Shukoh's troops, under the command of
Dara's elder son, Sulayman Shukoh, near Benares and was badly
beaten. According to one report, so much blood was spilled that
the battlegrounds glistened like a field of red tulips. In May of

Figure 2. Emperor Aurangzeb in a Shaft of Light. Attributed to Hunhar, c. 1660. From The St. Petersburg Album, Freer Gallery of Art. Purchase—Charles Lang Freer Endowment, F1996.1.

1658 Aurangzeb sent Shuja a letter promising him an expanded role in administering the eastern portion of Aurangzeb's empire, but only if Shuja would stand down. Shuja rebuffed the offer and prepared for war.

Aurangzeb and Shah Shuja met on the battlefield at Khajwa, northwest of Allahabad, in January of 1659. Despite the last-minute desertion of Jaswant Singh, a Rajput previously loyal to Shah Jahan, Aurangzeb's army outnumbered Shuja's by more than two to one. The fight was fierce nonetheless. At one point Aurangzeb reportedly ordered the legs of his elephant tied together in order to prevent the beast from fleeing. Aurangzeb's resilience fortified his men, and they defeated Shuja's troops, prompting Shuja himself to run. For the next year and a half, Aurangzeb's army drove Shuja farther and farther east until the prince abandoned India altogether. In May of 1660 Shah Shuja set sail from Dacca with his family and disappeared into Burma, where he soon met his death at the hands of the ruler of Arakan, who possibly feared that the Mughal prince would lead a coup (the evidence for the source of the conflict and how Shuja died are murky).

Back in India the last major battle in the succession struggle took place over three days in March of 1659. Dara Shukoh entrenched a twenty-thousand-man army (largely recruited in Gujarat) in the hills outside of Ajmer, hoping that the terrain, along with defense walls and trenches, would favor his outnumbered forces. Aurangzeb initiated the conflict with an artillery barrage that lasted nearly two days and blanketed the entire area in dense smoke. In the words of Aurangzeb's court historian, "Gunpowder smoke hung over the battlefield like a storm cloud heavy with lightning. Struck with such sparks, the ground lit up, as if under the power of the philosopher's stone."

On the third day, Aurangzeb concentrated his assault on one wing of Dara's army. Most of the imperial forces attacked from the front while a contingent snuck up behind, turning the tide in Aurangzeb's favor. Stationed behind his army, Dara watched the vicious slaughter and then once again fled for his life.

Dara Shukoh ran for three months before he made the mistake of seeking refuge with Malik Jiwan, an Afghan chieftain whose life Dara had saved years earlier by begging for mercy from Shah Jahan. Not one for sentiment, Malik Jiwan briskly arrested Dara and sent him to Delhi as Aurangzeb's prisoner.

Life and Death

An emperor ought to stand midway between gentleness and severity.

—Aurangzeb

Aurangzeb celebrated his second coronation ceremony on June 15, 1659, nearly one year after he had first proclaimed himself head of the Mughal Empire. This time, the festivities were an extravagant display of Mughal wealth. Legions of singers proclaimed Aurangzeb's greatness, musicians received trays of gems, and so much cloth was used that "merchants belonging to the seven climes reaped enormous profits." Coins were struck and the Friday sermon read in the name of Aurangzeb Alamgir, the throne-adorning seizer of the world.

Aurangzeb, now forty years old, settled into his new role as emperor by dealing with the messy aftermath of his contested rise to power. The first loose end to tie up was Dara Shukoh, the previous heir apparent and Aurangzeb's most formidable foe throughout the succession struggle.

When Dara Shukoh arrived in Delhi a prisoner late in the summer of 1659, Aurangzeb ordered him and Dara's younger son, the fourteen-year-old Sipihr Shukoh, dressed in rags and paraded through the streets. The two defeated men wound through Delhi on an uncovered, mangy elephant, roasting under the scorching September sun, a sorry sight for all to behold. Behind them loomed a soldier, his sword drawn in case either attempted a desperate escape. Mughal subjects had witnessed demeaning displays before. A year and a half earlier Dara Shukoh had some of Shah Shuja's men marched through Agra in disgrace. But subjecting Mughal princes to such disparaging treatment was something else entirely. Francois Bernier reported that the gathered crowds recoiled at the public humiliation of Dara Shukoh and his teenage son.

The following day, Dara Shukoh was beheaded on Aurangzeb's direct command. Some contemporary sources mentioned that Aurangzeb cited Dara's alleged apostasy from Islam to justify the death sentence, whereas others simply noted the execution. A few years later Aurangzeb put Murad to death on the pretense of retribution for a prior murder. It seems that Aurangzeb preferred to rationalize killing his brothers, no matter how flimsy the charges. Perhaps such explanations were important for a king who grounded his rule on dispensing justice. For Sulayman Shukoh, the elder of Dara's two sons, however, Aurangzeb did not bother with such guises and ordered him overdosed on opium water in 1661.

While Aurangzeb's murderous actions no doubt strike modern readers as harsh, his brothers would not have acted any differently. Manucci captured this dynamic when he reported that, on the day of his death, Dara Shukoh was asked by Aurangzeb what he would do if their roles were reversed. Seeing the writing on the wall, Dara sneered that he would have Aurangzeb's body quartered and displayed on Delhi's four main gates. While he shared his brother's visceral hatred, Aurang-

zeb exercised restraint by comparison. Aurangzeb ordered Dara
Shukoh's corpse buried at Humayun's tomb in Delhi, where it
rests today.

.   .   .

Following strong Mughal precedents, Aurangzeb showed leniency, even consideration, to most former supporters of Dara
Shukoh and his other brothers. He welcomed his brothers'
troops and their chief advisers within his own army and administration without reprisals. He repaid the loans that Murad had
taken from the prosperous Gujarati Jain merchant Shantidas. In
the 1670s Aurangzeb even married his daughter Zubdatunnisa
to Sipihr Shukoh, the younger of Dara Shukoh's sons, and wed-
ded his son Prince Akbar to Sulayman Shukoh's daughter. Only
a few of Dara Shukoh's circle were not shown mercy, such as
Sarmad, an Armenian Jewish mystic known for being irreverent
who had prophesied that Dara Shukoh would take the throne.
Aurangzeb executed Sarmad in 1661.

Aurangzeb took a more cutting approach to Dara Shukoh's
cultural legacy. During his decades at Shah Jahan's court in the
1640s and 1650s, Dara Shukoh enjoyed ample time to devote to
religious, literary, and spiritual pursuits. He ordered a team of
Brahmins to render fifty *Upanishad*s into Persian, a translation
that later found its way to France and introduced Europe to
this body of Sanskrit works. He held philosophical conversations with Baba Lal, a Punjabi spiritual leader. Dara composed
the *Confluence of Two Oceans*, a Persian treatise contending that
Hinduism and Islam lead to the same goal (the treatise was
translated into Sanskrit under the title *Samudrasangama*).

Faced with this strong interest in Hindu philosophy, especially Sanskrit texts, on the part of the previous heir apparent,
Aurangzeb introduced a clear rupture. He discontinued Dara

Shukoh's cross-cultural activities and severed the one lingering tie between Shah Jahan and the Sanskrit cultural world by
cutting off the imperial stipend to Kavindracarya Sarasvati, a
Brahmin from Benares. Kavindracarya lobbied Aurangzeb to
reinstate the stipend but was unsuccessful. In such acts Aurangzeb sought to separate himself from the cultural interests of his
eldest brother.

.   .   .

Dealing with Dara Shukoh and his legacy was child's play
compared to the looming question of Shah Jahan, who had recovered his health by the time Aurangzeb took the throne. In
essence, Aurangzeb locked away his father in Agra's Red Fort—
some whimsically say with a tantalizing view of his beloved Taj
Mahal—and threw away the key. The fifth Mughal king spent
his final seven and half years of life under house arrest, often
in the company of Jahanara, his eldest daughter. Many decried
Shah Jahan's dethronement and imprisonment, however, and
the tragedy of his jailed father vexed Aurangzeb during his
early years of rule.

While it was an accepted Mughal practice for brothers to
fight for the throne, overthrowing one's reigning father was
considered abhorrent. The chief qazi (Muslim judge) of the
Mughal Empire felt so strongly on the matter that he risked
imperial wrath and refused to endorse Aurangzeb's ascension
while Shah Jahan lived. Aurangzeb dismissed him and hired a
more pliable man for the job, Abdul Wahhab.

Far beyond India, too, many censured Aurangzeb for his
brutality against Shah Jahan. The sharif of Mecca declined to
recognize Aurangzeb as the proper ruler of Hindustan and even
refused his financial gifts for several years over Shah Jahan's
mistreatment. Playing on Aurangzeb's regnal title of Alamgir

(World Seizer), the Safavid king Shah Sulayman (r. 1666–94) wrote a caustic letter accusing Aurangzeb of mistakenly announcing his seizure of the world (*alam-giri*) when he had merely seized his father (*pidar-giri*). Aurangzeb retorted by touting his merciful termination of numerous taxes (some sources say eighty in all) upon his ascension as a mark of his just posture. But Aurangzeb's only response to the accusation that he overthrew his father was sheer denial; he claimed to Shah Sulayman (falsely) that Shah Jahan had voluntarily retired and conferred the crown on Aurangzeb.

Aurangzeb never fully came to terms with his unjust handling of his father. This rocky start haunted him throughout his rule and even shaped his piety, as we will see. This early moment also marked a key characteristic of Aurangzeb's commitment to justice, namely that it was limited by ambition. During his long reign Aurangzeb faced numerous conflicts between his principles and his politics, and the former rarely won out.

·   ·   ·

In spite of his detractors and bumpy beginning, Aurangzeb ruled the Mughal Empire for forty-nine years, until his death in 1707. He faced periodic rebellions, like all Mughal sovereigns, but he was a resilient king.

CHAPTER 3

The Grand Arc of Aurangzeb's Reign

Expansion and Justice

I wish you to recollect that the greatest conquerors are not always the
greatest kings. The nations of the earth have often been subjugated by mere
uncivilised barbarians, and the most extensive conquests have in a few short
years crumbled to pieces. He is the truly great king who makes it the chief
business of his life to govern his subjects with equity.

—*Aurangzeb, writing to the recently dethroned Shah Jahan*

Aurangzeb inherited a wealthy, thriving, expansionist empire.
Mughal state revenues had increased under his father, Shah
Jahan. Shah Jahan was also known for his building projects,
having financed the Taj Mahal in Agra and Shahjahanabad in
Delhi. Aurangzeb's forte, however, lay with the extension of
imperial borders.

Throughout his reign Aurangzeb crushed rebellions, waged
cold-blooded wars of expansion, and oversaw merciless sieges.
He was often happy to use diplomacy to extend and solidify
Mughal power, especially in the first half of his reign (1658–81).
But Aurangzeb did not hesitate to resort to force to enlarge
Mughal domains. For example, in the 1660s Aurangzeb tried
to lure the Maratha leader Shivaji into imperial service in
order to neutralize the Maratha threat to the Mughal state.
When that effort failed, Aurangzeb turned to violence and
fought the Marathas, with limited success, for the rest of his
life. Aurangzeb also punished those he believed had helped

Shivaji escape from Mughal clutches, destroying temples in Benares and Mathura.

Aurangzeb faced numerous other armed threats to the integrity of the Mughal Empire in the first half of his rule and showed little clemency. For instance, he had the Sikh guru Tegh Bahadur executed in 1675 for taking up arms against the Mughal state. The Rathor and Sisodia Rajputs rebelled in the late 1670s, and Aurangzeb used military force to compel both groups to return to the imperial fold. Aurangzeb struck hard against family members who compromised state interests. For instance, Aurangzeb's son, Prince Akbar, rebelled in 1681 and was chased to the Deccan and soon forced to flee to Iran—where he died in 1704—in order to escape his father's wrath.

.   .   .

In 1681 Aurangzeb took the unprecedented step of relocating south, along with his entire royal court, in order to lead the imperial absorption of the Deccan. The Mughals had pursued control over the Deccan since the days of Akbar, Aurangzeb's great-grandfather. Some emperors had made inroads down south, but Aurangzeb was the first to extend Mughal power across most of the Deccan.

Aurangzeb spent the second half of his reign (1681–1707) in south India, growing the Mughal kingdom to its greatest extent. He besieged Bijapur and Golconda in the 1680s, prompting both sultanates to fold. During the 1690s and 1700s he seized numerous hill forts as far south as Tamil Nadu from the clutches of Marathas. By the time of Aurangzeb's death, in 1707, the population of the Mughal kingdom was double that of contemporary Europe, and Mughal landholdings reached an all-time high.

In his bent for war and power Aurangzeb differed little

from his forebears, although he exhibited notable ambition and success. The weight of upholding a unified Mughal Empire and, where possible, expanding its borders rested heavily on Aurangzeb's shoulders and molded his aggressive military ventures. But inhabiting the Mughal throne involved far more than shedding blood and drawing ever widening lines on a map. For Aurangzeb, a preoccupation with dispensing justice (*'adl*) existed alongside his thirst for earthly power.

.   .   .

At times Aurangzeb claimed that being a fair, ethical ruler ranked above controlling territory, a surprising hierarchy to find embraced by the head of an expansionist state. Once, the deposed Shah Jahan criticized his newly crowned son for ineffectively deploying troops in the Deccan and Bengal. Aurangzeb retorted that skilled conquerors are not always skilled rulers, whose primary purpose is just governance.

Aurangzeb's professed devotion to justice finds substantial support among many contemporary sources. For instance, the Italian traveler Niccoli Manucci, no Aurangzeb enthusiast, spoke of the king: "He was of a melancholy temperament, always busy at something or another, wishing to execute justice and arrive at appropriate decisions." Ishvaradasa, a Hindu astrologer, wrote about Aurangzeb in Sanskrit in 1663 and called the king righteous (*dharmya*) and even noted that his tax policies were lawful (*vidhivat*).

Aurangzeb's entire ethos of sovereignty was infused with his fixation on justice, albeit sprinkled with healthy doses of a knack for devious politicking and an unquenchable thirst for power. Accordingly, if we are to understand anything about Aurangzeb's life and reign—from his trampling on his brothers for the throne of Hindustan to his treatment of Hindu temples to his burial at a Sufi shrine—we must reconstruct what he thought it meant to be an effective, equitable leader. Especially instructive are cases where Aurangzeb went against his ideals regarding ethics and justice, such as overthrowing his father and waging brutal wars against Muslim kingdoms in the Deccan. Aurangzeb was often deeply troubled by his actions that were motivated by realpolitik, and his discomfort points up both the depth and limits of his commitment to just rule.

Heir of the Grand Mughal Tradition

In the region of Hindustan, this scrap of bread [i.e., the Mughal Empire] is a generous gift from Their Majesties, Timur and Akbar.

—Aurangzeb, letter to his grandson Bidar Bakht

Alongside an empire, Aurangzeb inherited an illustrious Mughal past that furnished rich role models and formidable responsibilities. In his writings he named key imperial ancestors as exemplars for how to be a great king. In a letter from late in his life, for example, Aurangzeb advised one of his grandsons that the Mughal Empire was a gift from Timur and Akbar that subsequent generations were charged with upholding in all its glory.

Through his ancestors, Aurangzeb was heir to a vast, varied set of Mughal cultural and social practices. For decades, Mughal kings had built magnificent buildings, patronized poets and scholars, maintained great libraries of manuscripts, fashioned elaborate court rituals, and supported painters and artisans. Aurangzeb perpetuated many of these artistic, intellectual, and architectural interests while discarding and modifying others. He never broke from his Mughal heritage, but he refined it into his own, distinctive creation.

·   ·   ·

Initially, Aurangzeb's cultural and courtly activities followed closely on the heels of Shah Jahan and earlier Mughal kings.

For example, during his first few years as king, Aurangzeb erected a monumental tomb in Aurangabad for his first wife, Dilras Banu Begum, who died in 1657 from complications following the birth of her fifth child. The shining white mausoleum, known as Bibi ka Maqbara (Queen's Tomb), mimics the appearance of Shah Jahan's Taj Mahal, although it is half the size and displays exteriors of burnished stucco rather than marble. Its derisive modern nickname, "poor man's Taj," hardly does justice to Aurangzeb's vision of honoring his wife with a classic Mughal tomb.

Throughout his first ten years on the throne, Aurangzeb upheld many Mughal imperial practices borrowed or derived from Hindu customs. The king appeared daily to his subjects in the jharoka palace window in order to give them a darshan, or auspicious glimpse, of his royal visage. On his solar and lunar birthdays he was publicly weighed against gold and silver that was distributed to the poor, a Hindu ritual that the Mughals had adopted in Akbar's days.

Aurangzeb maintained personal contacts with Hindu religious figures. For instance, he penned a letter to Mahant Anand Nath in 1661 requesting a medicinal preparation from the yogi. In the 1660s he increased Anand Nath's landholdings in a village in the Punjab. Such connections echoed Jahangir's meetings with the Hindu ascetic Jadrup and Akbar's land grants to Vaishnava communities in Mathura.

For years Aurangzeb's pleasure activities also copied those of his ancestors. He summered in Kashmir, a favorite playground of the Mughal kings, and enjoyed music. The king had expert knowledge of the art of music according to Bakhtawar Khan, a little cited but important historian of the period. A musical treatise dated to 1666, Faqirullah's *Rag Darpan*, listed the names of Aurangzeb's favorite singers and instrumentalists.

.   .   .

In the second decade of his reign Aurangzeb began to alter his royal behavior. He rolled back some of his court rituals with Hindu roots and withdrew imperial patronage from certain practices, such as music. He also eliminated the position of formal court historian. These changes resulted in a more austere environment at Aurangzeb's court, although little changed elsewhere in the Mughal Empire.

Until 1668 Aurangzeb supported an official chronicler, Muhammad Kazim, who enjoyed access to the Mughal library and official documents. Mughal kings did not always employ formal historians; Babur and Jahangir penned their own memoirs, and the major histories of Humayun's reign were written after his death. But Akbar and Shah Jahan, arguably the two main paradigms among prior Mughal kings for Aurangzeb, generally kept historians on their payrolls. Aurangzeb broke with this precedent when, upon receiving Muhammad Kazim's *Alamgirnama* (History of Aurangzeb Alamgir) that covered the first ten regnal years, he reassigned the author to other tasks.

Aurangzeb's reasons for hardening his heart against his court chronicler remain unclear. Numerous scholars have tried to solve the riddle of Aurangzeb's sudden distaste for official history, hypothesizing that he elected to focus on esoteric rather than external things, the king became too pious to fund non-theological texts, or the royal treasury was strapped. All of these theories are unlikely given subsequent events at the royal court. In any case Aurangzeb never appointed another court historian, although he also did not ban history writing, as some twentieth-century scholars have suggested based on faulty readings of later chronicles. Numerous Mughal officials wrote Persian-language histories during or shortly after Aurangzeb's reign that have come down to us today.

Aurangzeb instituted several alterations to court protocol in the late 1660s. He ceased appearing to his subjects in a daily royal darshan in 1669. Around the same time, he reportedly cancelled his birthday weighings against gold and silver. He pulled musicians from many public court rituals and assigned them to other tasks (at enhanced salaries, curiously).

Some of these shifts likely stemmed from savvy statesmanship. For instance, cancelling daily attendance at the jharoka window may well have staved off imperial unrest. When Shah Jahan fell ill in 1657, news of his affliction was impossible to contain because of his sudden absence from the jharoka. Even though Shah Jahan was only bedridden for ten days, that was long enough to set in motion the wheels of Mughal princely conflict.

But not all of Aurangzeb's changes around the ten-year mark of his reign can be explained as prudent policies. His turn against music, for instance, seemed to lack a practical benefit and was instead likely a matter of evolving personal tastes. He perhaps felt similarly about being weighed against precious metals, although he arguably changed his mind in subsequent decades. Later in life, Aurangzeb recommended the weighing rites to his grandson Bidar Bakht and may even have resumed them himself, according to the 1690 report of the European traveler John Ovington. Aurangzeb did not rekindle his earlier zeal for music, but, in a late letter, he advised his son that it was a proper royal activity. Nonetheless, one net effect of these combined shifts around 1669 is undeniable: Aurangzeb stripped his court of numerous hallmarks of Mughal culture, including several rituals with Hindu roots.

A second, perhaps unforeseen, consequence of Aurangzeb's new policies was that they disseminated talent to the courts of his sons and Mughal nobles. For example, Aurangzeb abstained from music, but some of his sons enthusiastically sponsored musicians and musical treatises. As Katherine Schofield has pointed out, authors produced more Indo-Persian treatises on music during Aurangzeb's rule than in the prior five hundred years of Indian history. Painting may well have taken a similar route. Circumstantial evidence suggests that Aurangzeb ceased regular funding to painters after the 1660s, but numerous images survive today of the emperor in his old age. Most likely, images of a seasoned Aurangzeb emerged from princely courts where Mughal painting traditions thrived. Persian poetry, too, flourished during this period, and Aurangzeb's own daughter, Zebunnisa, was a notable poet who wrote under the penname *Makhfi* (hidden one).

Aurangzeb's earlier turn against Sanskrit pandits also dispersed talent to subimperial patrons. For example, after losing his imperial stipend on Aurangzeb's orders in the late 1650s Kavindracarya found employment in the court of Danishmand Khan, a Mughal noble, and later assisted the French traveler Francois Bernier. Shaysta Khan, Aurangzeb's maternal uncle, was a noted patron of Sanskrit intellectuals and Sanskrit-related projects. While governor of Bengal, he directed Basant Rae to compose a table of contents for the Persian *Mahabharata* translated under Akbar. Shaysta Khan even personally composed verses of Sanskrit poetry that are preserved today in the *Rasakalpadruma* (Wishing tree of aesthetic emotion). For their part, Sanskrit poets never ceased to recognize Aurangzeb. For instance, Devadatta, author of the *Gujarishatakam* on the dalliances of Gujarati women, mentioned Aurangzeb and his son Azam Shah in the work's opening lines.

.   .   .

Aurangzeb's court had a different feel after 1669, appearing less exuberant in some respects. But many things nonetheless signaled continuity with Mughal culture under Shah Jahan, including formal court rituals and royal patronage.

European travelers described the elaborate proceedings of Aurangzeb's court, which was governed by strict rules and regulations. The emperor sat on an elevated platform and, when in Delhi, on the Peacock Throne, which had more jewels than those in courtly attendance could count. The king adorned himself with silk, a turban woven in gold, and pearls and jewels aplenty. Nobles stood, arrayed by their rank in the Mughal hierarchy, and gazed up at this glittering display. Sumptuous carpets covered the floors, and woven fabrics draped the walls. The imperial band (*naubat*), which was not subject to Aurangzeb's restrictions on music, stood at the ready. In this luxurious environment Aurangzeb gave and received gifts, welcomed visitors and nobles, and carried out government business.

The 1670s witnessed a few large-scale imperial projects that were in line with earlier Mughal culture but also bore the imprint of Aurangzeb's own interests. At court, for instance, Muslim scholars completed the massive intellectual project *Fatawa-i Alamgiri*, a synthesis of Hanafi legal judgments, in 1675 after eight years of labor. During its compilation Aurangzeb heard parts of the work read aloud and even offered corrections. Thereafter judges across the empire drew from the book, originally mainly in Arabic but immediately translated into Persian. The religious edge to this text perhaps reflected Aurangzeb's piety, and the king's preoccupation with justice may have inspired him to provide a clear legal code. But the broader Mughal commitment to sweeping scholarly projects runs smoothly from Akbar through Aurangzeb. Also like his forefathers, Aurangzeb sup-

ported a vast imperial library and even spent one million rupees
to preserve his manuscript collection.

In the mid-1670s Aurangzeb sponsored the construction
of the monumental Badshahi Masjid in Lahore (fig. 3). Unlike with Dilras's "poor man's Taj," here Aurangzeb approached
Shah Jahan's genius. Aurangzeb's flagship mosque features
floral motifs, inlaid marble, cusped arches, and other elegant
touches. At the time it was built, the Badshahi Masjid was the
largest mosque in the world, and its expansive size—it can hold
sixty thousand people—still impresses modern visitors. The
building took some damage over the years and was repurposed
for artillery storage in the early nineteenth century by Ranjit
Singh, founder of the Sikh Empire. Today it again functions as
a mosque and awes onlookers with its profound beauty, evocative of Mughal aesthetic tastes.

.   .   .

Figure 3. Badshahi Masjid in Lahore. Photo by the author.

Aurangzeb left Delhi in 1679 and never returned to north India. From 1681 onward he moved around the Deccan, tirelessly campaigning and living out of a vast assemblage of red tents. Aurangzeb's ancestors had often camped in tents—colored red as a mark of Mughal royalty—so here, too, Aurangzeb followed an inherited tradition. As Mughal life returned to its nomadic roots, Aurangzeb emphasized his own priorities and tastes, which included many trademark features of high Mughal culture.

Throughout his half century of rule, for example, Aurangzeb held formal court daily and, at times, twice daily. He prided himself on dispensing justice and often personally wrote out answers to petitions. The emperor maintained ties to astrologers, a critical aspect of Mughal kingship, even into the eighteenth century. Gemelli Careri, an Italian visitor to India in the 1690s, wrote that "King [Aurangzeb] undertakes nothing without the advice of his astrologers." In 1707, shortly before Aurangzeb's death, a court astrologer recommended that the emperor cure a fever by giving away an elephant and diamond. Aurangzeb rejected this advice as inappropriately following the shared Hindu and Parsi custom of gifting an elephant in charity, although he did order the distribution of four thousand rupees to the poor. It is notable that forty-nine years into his reign such an astrologer had access to the emperor.

More generally, Aurangzeb's later years were far from devoid of the Hindu ideas, texts, and culture that had become an integrated part of Mughal imperial life long before his rule. For example, in the early 1690s a poet by the name of Chandraman dedicated his *Nargisistan* (Narcissus garden), a Persian poetic retelling of the *Ramayana*, to Aurangzeb. In 1705 Amar Singh followed suit, dedicating his prose Persian *Ramayana* (titled

Amar Prakash) to Aurangzeb. Akbar had sponsored the first Persian *Ramayana*, one of the two great Sanskrit epics and a key theological text for many Hindus by this period, in the late sixteenth century. During the next hundred years poets composed numerous distinct Persian *Ramayana*s, and many dedicated their works to the reigning Mughal king. Even at the end of his reign, Aurangzeb had not moved so far afield from Mughal cultural practices as to break the perceived association between Mughal royalty and the epic Hindu tale of Ram.

CHAPTER 4

Administrator of Hindustan

Watching Over His Vast Empire

Shah Jahan used to hold court one day a week and owing to the cherishing of truth and devotion to God, nobody had need to lodge a complaint. Now Emperor Aurangzeb holds court twice daily and the crowd of complaints grows greater.

—*Bhimsen Saxena, a Hindu member of Aurangzeb's administration, writing in Persian*

Aurangzeb oversaw a vast kingdom that required a vast bureaucratic apparatus. He was not a regular presence in most parts of the empire but rather spent the first half of his reign mainly at court in Delhi and the second half campaigning in the Deccan. Accordingly, state officials shouldered the daily work of running the Mughal Empire. Aurangzeb's physical distance did not prevent him from becoming personally involved with many administrative details, however, in his persistent but elusive pursuit of justice.

Aurangzeb kept apprised of happenings from the four corners of his kingdom by prolific news bulletins (*akhbarat*) that arrived daily and reported on princely courts, the activities of state officials, and noteworthy events. All leaders of the time relied on such news bulletins, which also relayed happenings at Aurangzeb's court to friends and foes across India. For example, Herbert de Jager, a Dutch envoy, reported that Shivaji was so

عالمگیر پادشاه

Figure 4. Portrait of the Emperor Aurangzeb, c. seventeenth century. Metropolitan Museum of Art, New York. Bequest of George D. Pratt, 1935, 45.174.28.

inundated with news reports and letters that he could barely spare the time for a meeting in 1677.

Aurangzeb was especially keen to hear reports on public law and order and the behavior of Mughal state representatives. These areas often exposed fault lines in Aurangzeb's attempts to rule an unwieldy empire.

. . .

Aurangzeb exhibited deep concern with basic security throughout Mughal territory. He repeatedly wrote to his sons and important nobles about ensuring the safety of the roads and chided them for failing to prevent theft and other crimes against ordinary subjects. Despite Aurangzeb's efforts, however, law-and-order problems afflicted Mughal India and possibly even worsened in the final years of his reign. By this point Mughal forces were stretched thin and wearied by decades of conflict. Many new recruits lacked loyalty to the Mughal cause. Writing in the mid-1690s, the Italian Gemelli Careri complained that Mughal India did not offer travelers "safety from thieves," unlike the comparatively secure roads in Safavid Iran and the Ottoman Empire. Aurangzeb himself lamented that bandits robbed travelers near major cities, such as Burhanpur and Ahmedabad, which meant that rural areas suffered even bolder attacks.

Aurangzeb also struggled to maintain control over his state officers, who were of mixed quality. Mughal administrators regularly accepted bribes, despite Aurangzeb's strict orders forbidding such corruption. Even Abdul Wahhab, the chief qazi and thus a moral guide of the empire, as an eighteenth-century Indo-Persian work put it, "had a long arm for hauling and snatching, and collected large sums of money." Delinquent administrators frustrated Aurangzeb, and the king condemned their unjust ways. For example, in a late letter to his grandson

Bidar Bakht, Aurangzeb mentioned a few corrupt nobles and then advised: "sovereignty does not stand absent punishment." But the emperor also showed his men leniency. He chastised his sons for imposing harsh reprimands on imperial officials and even commuted such sentences.

. . .

Aurangzeb's clemency often did not extend to family members. He penalized relations who opposed state interests and even those who simply made mistakes. This proclivity reared its head during the war of succession and continued throughout his reign.

For example, Aurangzeb sent his uncle Shaysta Khan south in 1659 to counter the military opposition mounted by Shivaji, a Maratha warrior who threatened Mughal interests in the Deccan. Shaysta Khan built lovely buildings and gardens in Pune and brought prosperity to the entire region. Grain prices remained low, and the people benefited from Shaysta Khan's generosity. Shaysta Khan, too, enjoyed a good life in Pune, busying himself with such matters as arranging his daughter's engagement. In all of this, however, Shaysta Khan lost sight of his major objective: reining in Shivaji.

But Shivaji did not forget Shaysta Khan and ambushed his palace in the spring of 1663. Shivaji took with him only a few dozen men who sneaked into the compound under the cover of night. When the Marathas burst into his bedroom, Shaysta Khan defended himself and lost a finger in the process. But he was unable to protect his family, and several of his wives perished. Shivaji and his troops retreated when, according to some reports, they slew Shaysta Khan's son in his bed, mistaking him for his father. Upon hearing of this shameful defeat, Aurangzeb packed his uncle off to Bengal, known as a backwater of the Mughal kingdom, without even allowing Shaysta Khan the courtesy of visiting his nephew the emperor on his way east.

In a less dramatic but illustrative incident decades later, Aurangzeb rebuked his son Azam Shah for not preventing robbery on the Surat highway. Azam protested that this was not his responsibility but rather fell within the jurisdiction of another official. In response, Aurangzeb reduced his son's *mansab* rank and noted, "If it had been an officer other than a Prince, this order would have been issued after an inquiry. For a Prince the punishment is the absence of investigation."

Aurangzeb acted even more severely when he faced a rebellion by his fourth son, Prince Akbar. Akbar declared himself emperor in 1681, after being dispatched by his father to put down a rebellion by the Rathors and Sisodias of Rajasthan. Akbar soon lost the support of his Rajput allies and fled to the court of Sambhaji, Shivaji's son and a sworn enemy of Aurangzeb by this point. After several years, in 1687, Aurangzeb drove his son out of India, and Prince Akbar absconded to Persia, where he died in 1704.

.   .   .

Aurangzeb did not tolerate threats to state security, and individuals who challenged the emperor often found themselves on the receiving end of his capacity for violence and even cruelty at times.

For example, Sambhaji received no mercy when he was captured by Mughal forces in 1689. Aurangzeb ordered Sambhaji, who had spent years fighting the Mughal state, along with his Brahmin adviser, Kavi Kalash, publicly humiliated by being forced to wear funny hats and being led into court on camels. He then had Sambhaji's eyes stabbed out with nails, and, in one historian's poetic words, "his shoulders were lightened

of the load of his head." Some histories add that the bodies of
Sambhaji and Kavi Kalash were thrown to the dogs while their
heads were stuffed with straw and displayed in cities throughout the Deccan before being hung on one of Delhi's gates.

Aurangzeb was not unusual for his time in turning to violence, including of a gruesome variety, as a standard political
tactic. For Aurangzeb state violence was not only permissible
but necessary and even just insofar as it encouraged stability and
cooperation within the Mughal kingdom. That Aurangzeb acted
as a man of his times regarding state force, however, has not
saved him from scathing condemnation by subsequent generations. One poignant example of Aurangzeb's violence that sits ill
with many today concerns Tegh Bahadur, the ninth Sikh guru.

The Mughal state executed Tegh Bahadur in 1675 for caus-
ing unrest in the Punjab. This incident is central to how many
modern Sikhs understand the early history of their religion,
but it was likely a more routine matter from a Mughal perspective. The execution is not mentioned in any Persian texts
from Aurangzeb's period, which suggests that it was not an
exceptional event for the Mughals. Later Persian works offer
conflicting reports on even basic details, such as the location of
Tegh Bahadur's execution (some name the Deccan or Lahore,
whereas others concur with the Sikh tradition that the killing
took place in Delhi). Sikh accounts of the execution also date
from a later period and vary considerably. The popular story,
often repeated in modern textbooks, that Tegh Bahadur was
protesting against the forced conversion of Kashmiri Brahmins
is not elaborated in the earliest sources on the execution.

This much is clear from both Persian and Sikh sources: In
Aurangzeb's eyes, Tegh Bahadur militarily opposed Mughal
state interests and so was a legitimate target for a death sen-

tence. His religious stature did nothing to mitigate the over-arching commitment of Aurangzeb's administration to meting out punishment, including capital punishment, to enemies of the state. It probably did not help matters that Tegh Bahadur's nephew and the seventh Sikh guru, Har Rai, was rumored to have supported Dara Shukoh during the war of succession. Around the same time, the Mughals targeted other religious groups that took up arms against the state, such as the Satnamis.

Prized Hindu Nobles

O King, may the world bow to your command;

May lips drip with expressions of thanks and salutations;

Since it is your spirit that watches over the people,

Wherever you are, may God watch over you!

—*Chandar Bhan Brahman, a Hindu, Persian-medium poet in Aurangzeb's employ*

Hindus fared well in Aurangzeb's massive bureaucracy, finding employment and advancement opportunities. Since Akbar's time, Rajputs and other Hindus had served as full members of the Mughal administration. Like their Muslim counterparts, they received formal ranks known as *mansab*s that marked their status in the imperial hierarchy and fought to expand the empire. Muslims numerically dominated the corps of the Mughal elite, but Hindus, too, occupied elevated positions and were entrusted with critical state business. In part, Aurangzeb pursued a practical strategy by incorporating Hindus into the Mughal bureaucracy, especially as he sought to win over hearts, minds, and territory in the Deccan. But in many cases Aurangzeb was unconcerned with the religious identity of his state officials, whom he selected primarily for their administrative skills.

When Shah Jahan's sons clashed in the war of succession

(1657–59), Hindu members of the Mughal administration split in their support of Aurangzeb versus Dara Shukoh. More Rajputs backed Dara, whereas more Marathas (who, by the mid-seventeenth century, had become a formidable constituency) sided with Aurangzeb. But taken as a whole, twenty-one high-ranking Hindu nobles (i.e., those with an imperial *mansab* rank exceeding one thousand) fought with Aurangzeb compared to twenty-four who championed Dara. In other words, Aurangzeb and Dara Shukoh garnered nearly equal support among Hindu nobles.

From the perspective of many Mughal elites, Hindu and Muslim alike, Aurangzeb was the smart bet to ascend the throne. Other Hindu members of the Mughal court, such as the poet Chandar Bhan Brahman, treated Aurangzeb's victory as an acceptable development that did not alter the basic core of the Mughal state.

As expected, Aurangzeb's ascension initially changed little about the Hindu share in Mughal administration. Under Akbar, for example, Hindus were 22.5 percent of all Mughal nobles. That percentage hardly budged in either direction under Shah Jahan, and, in the first twenty-one years of Aurangzeb's reign (1658–79), it stayed level at 21.6 percent. But between 1679 and 1707 Aurangzeb increased Hindu participation at the elite levels of the Mughal state by nearly 50 percent. Hindus rose to 31.6 percent of the Mughal nobility. This dramatic rise featured a substantial influx of Marathas as a strategic aspect of expanding Mughal sovereignty across the Deccan.

Beyond the numbers, individual stories capture the tale of prized Hindu nobles in Aurangzeb's India, such as that of Raja Raghunatha.

·   ·   ·

Raja Raghunatha was one of Aurangzeb's most cherished state officers, even though he served the king for a mere five years. Raghunatha began his imperial career as a financial minister in Shah Jahan's government. After Aurangzeb routed Dara Shukoh at Samugarh, Raghunatha joined a group of administrators who pledged loyalty to Aurangzeb.

Aurangzeb appointed Raghunatha his diwani, the chief finance minister of the empire. This high position mirrored Akbar's appointment of Todar Mal as his top finance minister one hundred years earlier. At his second coronation ceremony Aurangzeb honored his Hindu diwani with the title of raja and raised his *mansab* rank to twenty-five hundred. Thereafter, Raghunatha ran the imperial treasury with an expert hand.

Within a few years, Raghunatha's influence at court outstripped even his high office, and the French traveler Bernier described him as acting vizier of the empire. Chandar Bhan agreed with this assessment and lauded Raghunatha as the "frontispiece in the book of the men of the pen of Hindustan." Raghunatha's life was cut short in 1663 while he accompanied Aurangzeb on a pleasure trip to enjoy the lush scenery of Kashmir, a favorite Mughal pastime. Aurangzeb did not forget his beloved Hindu diwani, however.

Even as an old man facing death decades later, Aurangzeb remembered and evoked his inaugural financial officer. In letters written to other administrators in his final years, Aurangzeb cited Raghunatha's advice on running an efficient government. For instance, writing to his vizier Asad Khan, Aurangzeb reported Raghunatha's sage guidance that "the work of government should be entrusted to people with prized experience and a head for business, not to those weak with greed." More than forty years after his death, Raghunatha still loomed large in his patron's mind as an authority on not only finances but general Mughal state affairs and justice. For Aurangzeb, Raghunatha's religious identity was irrelevant to his memorialized status as a great officer of the Mughal Empire.

.   .   .

In the latter half of his reign Aurangzeb appointed Hindus within the imperial bureaucracy at an accelerated rate, even while he received pushback against the practice.

As I have noted, Hindu representation among Mughal officials rose by half between 1679 and 1707. Some people expressed reservations about this surge in Hindu nobles. For example, Bhimsen Saxena, a Hindu soldier who spent decades in Aurangzeb's employ and later wrote a history of the period in Persian, attested that "it was a practice in those days that the names of the Hindus were never recommended [for promotion]." Quite possibly rising numbers of Marathas—to the extent that they outnumbered Rajputs among Mughal nobles—unsettled other groups within the nobility and prompted an attempted (if failed) scaling-back in Hindu officers across the board.

Even in later years, however, Aurangzeb persisted in his view that there ought to be no religious litmus test for Mughal employment. One time, a Muslim from Bukhara who entered Mughal service in the late 1680s petitioned the emperor to deny imperial advancement to Persians on the grounds that they were Shias, not Sunnis. Aurangzeb rejected the proposal and opined, "What connection have earthly affairs with religion? And what right have administrative works to meddle with bigotry? 'For you is your religion and for me is mine.' If this rule [suggested by you] were established, it would be my duty to extirpate all the (Hindu) Rajahs and their followers. Wise men disapprove of the removal from office of able officers."

Maratha and Rajput Resistance

A governorship from Delhi is like an enticing prostitute.

Seeing her beauty, who doesn't long to possess her?

Her manner is to conquer the world by the power of trickery.

Whomever she approaches she immediately renders penniless.

Bhushan says, spending time in her company brings no reward.

—*Bhushan Tripathi, a Hindi poet working under Shivaji, 1673*

Not all Hindu elites enjoyed rosy relations with Aurangzeb. Rajputs had long served the Mughals, but from the moment they were first incorporated into the state under Akbar, periodic rebellions were de rigueur. Marathas, too, played both sides of the field, accepting and opposing Mughal rule at different moments.

Shivaji Bhonsle mounted the most famous opposition to Aurangzeb's expansionist agenda. Shivaji was a Maratha warrior and, eventually, a self-made king. He was born to a low-caste family and later underwent an elaborate Brahmin-led ritual to become a Rajput, a Kshatriya who could legitimately lead an independent state (Shivaji's state propaganda pitched this as recovering his forgotten Rajput lineage). Shivaji created significant problems for Aurangzeb, and the Mughal king tried for decades, largely unsuccessfully, to quell the Maratha warrior's destructive assaults on imperial strongholds.

Shivaji was a thorn in Aurangzeb's side even before Aurangzeb ascended the throne. Shivaji spent the 1650s carving a state out of the rolling hills of the western Deccan, near modern-day Pune. He first resisted Aurangzeb directly in 1657 when the prince was directing Shah Jahan's Deccan campaigns. When Aurangzeb abruptly left central India in order to fight for the Mughal throne, Shivaji took the opportunity to seize further territory.

By the 1660s, Shivaji commanded a force of ten thousand cavalry and fifty thousand infantry, which he deployed against Mughal targets. Shivaji was a master of guerilla warfare and raids, much more adept at nimble operations than the bulky Mughal army. I have already described, for instance, how in April of 1663 he infiltrated the house of Shaysta Khan, Aurangzeb's maternal uncle, in Pune with only a few dozen men and killed several of Shaysta Khan's wives and his son. In January of 1664 Shivaji raided Surat, one of the busiest ports on the western coast, with a population of two hundred thousand, and plundered the city for days while its Mughal governor cowered in a nearby fort.

Unable to bear such humiliations and breaches of state security, in early 1665 Aurangzeb ordered Mirza Raja Jai Singh to pursue Shivaji. Jai Singh, leader of the Kachhwaha Rajputs and a Hindu, was one of the chief Rajputs who supported Aurangzeb in the war of succession. After being besieged by Jai Singh in the Purandar hill fort for two months, Shivaji surrendered. He agreed to become a vassal of the Mughal state, turning over land and forts, paying tribute, and fighting for the Mughals. While he made a show of submission and cooperation, Shivaji's opposition to the Mughals was only beginning.

·   ·   ·

Shivaji visited Aurangzeb's court at Agra in May of 1666. He offered the Mughal emperor gifts and bowed in submission, as was expected for a recent foe-turned-noble, but relations soon soured. Many historians of the period narrated this encounter, the only recorded face-to-face meeting between Aurangzeb and Shivaji, but they spun different versions of the tale. Most agreed that Shivaji was upset at some perceived slight—perhaps not being acknowledged by the emperor or being asked to stand with lower-ranked nobles—and caused a ruckus at open court. One historian noted that Shivaji fell to the ground howling like a wounded animal, and another reported that he raved like a madman. Aurangzeb did not tolerate such violations of protocol, so Shivaji was escorted out of court and placed under house arrest.

Not long after his outburst, Shivaji fled from Agra along with his nine-year-old son, Sambhaji. Most likely Shivaji bribed their guards to let them out, although more fanciful versions of the story imagine them slipping away in large baskets meant to contain alms for Brahmins. Shivaji masqueraded as a wandering ascetic until he was clear of Mughal territory, and his young son adopted a similar disguise or, according to one historian, dressed as a Brahmin's wife in order to travel undetected. In 1669 Shivaji renewed his flagrant denial of Mughal authority by launching fresh attacks to regain forts he had surrendered a few years earlier.

Whatever the precise details of how the relationship went wrong, Aurangzeb failed to incorporate Shivaji into the Mughal fold. At first glance this failure may seem puzzling because generations of Rajputs had responded well to integration within the Mughal nobility. In this instance, however, lumping all Hindus together prevents us from seeing crucial differences that explain why Shivaji balked at his reception by Aurangzeb. Many Rajputs of the day looked down on Shivaji as an uncouth upstart who, in Mughal terms, was deficient in *adab* (proper conduct). Indeed, unlike most Rajputs, Shivaji lacked exposure to Persianate court culture. His father was a noble under the Adil Shahi dynasty of Bijapur, but Shivaji had been raised by his mother, Jijabai, without access to courtly life. Perhaps because of his background, not to mention his justified faith in his own acumen on the battlefield, Shivaji did not ease into his role as a Mughal noble, as many Rajputs had, and instead chose to fight Aurangzeb.

.   .   .

Shivaji's return to insurgency was devastating for the Mughals. Beginning in 1670 Shivaji plundered Surat and other places repeatedly. For the next four years he raided Mughal strongholds north of Maharashtra, such as Khandesh, Berar, and Baglan, and met opposition from imperial and Bijapuri troops alike. During this time Aurangzeb was largely occupied with putting down Pathan tribal revolts in the northwest mountainous regions of the empire.

In June of 1674, while Aurangzeb was leading an army into the mountains near the Khyber Pass in pursuit of the Afridi tribe, Shivaji crowned himself monarch or chhatrapati of an independent Maratha kingdom that stretched across parts of the Western Ghats and the Konkan coast. The full ceremonies took weeks to perform, and the coronation itself lasted nine days. There was little immediate precedent for such a rite, which included Shivaji "reclaiming" his alleged Kshatriya ancestry. Gagabhatta, a prominent Brahmin from Benares, wrote much of the ritual manual from scratch.

Shivaji spent the next six years expanding Maratha domains. He also directed further projects that sought, like his 1674 coronation, to replace Indo-Persian political norms with Sanskrit-based ones. For instance, in 1677 he sponsored a Sanskrit text known as *Rajavyavaharakosha* (Lexicon of royal institutes), which provided Sanskrit synonyms for fifteen hundred Indo-Persian administrative terms. Such a work may seem pedantic, but it helped Shivaji in his quest to subvert Mughal ruling culture. The later years of Shivaji's reign were marked by a significant uptick in Sanskrit terms in official Maratha documents.

Shivaji began experiencing bouts of illness in 1678 and died, in his bed, two years later in 1680. Rumors flew about regarding Shivaji's demise, including that his second wife, Sorayabai, poisoned her husband so that she could put her ten-year-old son, Rajaram, on the throne in lieu of Sambhaji, Shivaji's son by his first wife. The poisoning story is likely untrue, but a brief succession struggle ensued between Rajaram and Sambhaji. Sambhaji won and succeeded his father in plaguing Mughal interests in the Deccan.

.   .   .

Although Shivaji and Aurangzeb met in person only once, at court in 1666, they despised each other. Bhushan, one of Shivaji's court poets, defamed Aurangzeb as Kumbhakarna, the gigantic, gluttonous demon from the *Ramayana*. Aurangzeb called Shivaji a "mountain rat," and Mughal sources give his name as Shiva, often accompanied by a curse but never with the honorific -ji. One early eighteenth-century historian of Aurangzeb's reign recorded the brusque chronogram for Shiva-ji's death date: "The infidel went to hell" (*kafir bi jahannum raft*).

The Mughal-Maratha conflict was shaped by a craving for raw power that demanded strategic, shifting alliances. Shivaji allied with numerous Islamic states, including Bijapur, Golconda, and even the Mughals when it suited him (sometimes against Hindu powers in south India). Shivaji welcomed Muslims within his army; he had qazis (Muslim judges) on his payroll, and Muslims ranked among some of his top commanders. Mughal alliances and the imperial army were similarly diverse, and Aurangzeb sent a Hindu, Jai Singh, to besiege Shivaji at Purandar. Modern suggestions that Marathas who resisted Mughal rule thought of themselves as "Hindus" defying "Muslim" tyranny are just that: modern. Religion cropped up in these

encounters, such as in Shivaji's preoccupation with being or becoming a Kshatriya. Neither Mughal nor Maratha writers shied
away from religiously tinged rhetoric in narrating this clash,
especially in later accounts. But, on the ground, a thirst for political power drove both the Maratha opposition to Aurangzeb's
rule and the Mughal response.

.   .   .

Aurangzeb also faced periodic opposition from Rajputs, as had
his imperial predecessors. One striking episode was when the
Rajput families of Marwar and Mewar rebelled in 1679–81, a
decision that led to different outcomes for the two kingdoms.
Trouble was spurred when Jaswant Singh Rathor died in December of 1678, and Aurangzeb tried to intervene in the succession of the Marwar state in southwestern Rajasthan. The
Rathor royal family did not appreciate Aurangzeb's meddling,
especially his suggestion of raising two infant Marwar princes
at the imperial court and his decision to send troops to occupy
Jodhpur. The neighboring Sisodia Rajputs of Mewar feared a
similar invasion and so allied with Marwar.

    Aurangzeb assigned his son Prince Akbar to suppress the
joint Rathor-Sisodia rebellion. Akbar succeeded but, sensing an
opportunity, solicited the support of the Rathors and Sisodias
and crowned himself emperor at Nadol, Rajasthan, in early January 1681. Imperial pressure soon forced Prince Akbar to shift
his rebellion further south. Meanwhile, another son of Aurangzeb, Azam Shah, negotiated a diplomatic settlement with the
Rajputs in June of 1681 known as the Treaty of Rajsamudra. The
treaty heralded a lasting and fruitful peace between Mewar and
the Mughal Empire. But Marwar experienced uprisings for
years, fueled by frustration over the transition to being under
direct imperial control.

This entire set of events is sometimes framed by modern historians as the "Rajput rebellion" and cast as Hindu hostility to Muslim rule. This communal reading is belied by the decision of both the Rathors and Sisodias to support Prince Akbar, a Muslim, not to mention their divergent reactions to the Treaty of Rajsamudra. Mewar accepted peace with Aurangzeb, whereas Marwar continued to buck under the Mughal yoke. This event was, in actuality, a power struggle, akin to numerous other rebellions—by Hindu and Muslim rulers alike—against Mughal rule over the centuries.

CHAPTER 5

Moral Man and Leader

Piety and Power

The Emperor [Aurangzeb] wrote a prayer and threw [it] into the [flooded] water. Immediately the water began to subside. The prayer of the God-devoted Emperor was accepted by God, and the world became composed again.

—*Bhimsen Saxena, a Hindu soldier in Aurangzeb's employ, writing in Persian*

Like every other Mughal ruler, Aurangzeb was born a Muslim and practiced his inherited religion throughout his life. It is impossible to know the inner thoughts of long-dead kings, but, based on actions, it appears that Aurangzeb was more pious than his imperial predecessors. He prayed with greater regularity than his forefathers, and he abstained from drink and opium, indulgences that had killed several male members of the Mughal family. In the 1660s Aurangzeb memorized the Quran. In his later years he sewed prayer caps and copied the Quran by hand, both pious pursuits.

But Aurangzeb's approach to religion was hardly puritanical. On the contrary, he consulted with prominent Hindu religious figures throughout his life, as had earlier Mughal kings. For example, in the 1680s Aurangzeb conducted a religious discussion with the Bairagi Hindu Shiv Mangaldas Maharaj and showered the saint with gifts. The king had strong links with Islamic Sufi communities, another time-honored Mughal tradition, as evidenced by his burial at a Chishti shrine in Maharashtra. An image of Aurangzeb depicts his visit, along with two of his sons, to the shrine of Muinuddin Chishti (d. 1236) in Ajmer, Rajasthan, probably around 1680 (fig. 5). Aurangzeb's interpretation of Islam also included many talismanic aspects. For instance, he once wrote out prayers and had them sewn to banners and standards that were carried into battle against enemies of the state.

Figure 5. Emperor Aurangzeb at the Shrine of Muinuddin Chishti in Ajmer, Rajasthan, c. early eighteenth century. Mead Art Museum, Amherst College. Gift of Dr. and Mrs. Frank L. Babbott (class of 1913), AC 1963.4.

Aurangzeb often performed his piety on a public stage for the benefit of both himself and others. For example, sewing prayers to battle standards ensured victory in his eyes and those of his troops. The king once threw a written prayer into flooded waters (which caused them to subside, according to Bhimsen Saxena). Another historian tells of how Aurangzeb dismounted during a military clash in order to pray as an expression of devotion that also buoyed his troops with the confidence that God was on their side. Aurangzeb wanted to be, and to be seen as, a good Muslim.

As a Muslim ruler, Aurangzeb's religious ideals demanded that he dispense justice and protect his citizens. As the king put it in a letter to his grandson Azimusshan, "You should consider the protection of the subjects as the source of happiness in this world and the next." But the emperor ran into repeated problems regarding his public relationship with Islam. When the two conflicted, Aurangzeb generally sacrificed religious obligations on the altar of state interests, although such decisions weighed heavily on his heart.

· · ·

Aurangzeb broke Islamic law when he deposed his father and imprisoned him for the better part of a decade. As I have mentioned, the sharif of Mecca stated this judgment clearly and rebuffed Aurangzeb's requests for recognition as the legitimate ruler of Hindustan while Shah Jahan lived. Aurangzeb never ceased soliciting the sharif of Mecca to change his mind, which suggests that it bothered the Mughal emperor to lack approval from Muslim religious leaders. The problem resolved itself when Shah Jahan died in 1666, but the intermediary seven and a half years of ruling in violation of Islamic principles took a toll on Aurangzeb.

A European traveler a few decades later opined that Aurangzeb's "rigorous abstinence," including from alcohol, was the king's penance for his earlier sins against his father. Whether this precise connection is accurate, being branded an illegitimate Muslim monarch likely prompted Aurangzeb to become more devout. Many of his more obvious pious pursuits, such as memorizing and copying the Quran, began in earnest after his ascension. Here, Aurangzeb's religiosity did not shape state policy so much as his kingly experiences inspired changes in his religious life.

Over the course of his reign numerous other clashes arose between Islamic religious ideals and Mughal state interests. Aurangzeb privileged the latter almost invariably. For instance, during the assault on Bijapur in 1686, a delegation of Bijapuri theologians pleaded with Aurangzeb to end the siege on the grounds that warring against fellow Muslims was unjust. Aurangzeb remained unmoved and persisted with his brutal tactics until Bijapur fell. The emperor then ordered some Bijapuri palace wall paintings wiped out, perhaps as a limp attempt to reassert the theological righteousness of the Mughal state by adhering to the hardline view that images are idolatrous.

When he thought it served imperial interests, Aurangzeb even compromised Islamic principles that he had earlier endorsed. For instance, in 1700 Mughal soldiers captured nine Hindus and four Muslims during the siege of Satara Fort, a Maratha stronghold. Following the *Fatawa-i Alamgiri*, a legal book that Aurangzeb had sponsored, a Mughal judge sentenced the Muslims to three years in prison and offered the Hindus a full pardon if they converted to Islam. Dissatisfied with such leniency, Aurangzeb ordered the judge to "decide the case in some other way, that control over the kingdom may not be lost." The rebels were all executed before sundown.

. . .

The ulama, the learned men of Islam, were not blind to Aurangzeb's willingness to disregard religious scruples when it suited
him. Accordingly, like earlier Mughal rulers, Aurangzeb clashed
with the ulama, especially in their role as qazis (Muslim judges),
throughout his reign. On seizing the throne, he named Abdul
Wahhab chief qazi because the prior chief would not overlook
the sin of overthrowing Shah Jahan. Decades later Aurangzeb
fell out with Shaykh al-Islam, Abdul Wahhab's son and another qazi, because he refused to sanction Mughal assaults that
sought to overthrow the Islamic kingdoms of Bijapur and Golconda and killed many Muslims. Shaykh al-Islam soon resigned
and went on hajj to Mecca, a time-honored Mughal method of
removing men who refused to toe the imperial line.

Dating back to Akbar's reign, the ulama were a key component in the balance of Mughal power. Akbar ridiculed the more
uptight members of this community and exiled certain vocal
individuals. Like Akbar, Aurangzeb was not above displacing
problematic members of the ulama, such as Shah Jahan's chief
qazi who refused to sanction Aurangzeb's ascension. But, when
possible, Aurangzeb took a softer approach of placating the
ulama, especially by providing them with income.

Aurangzeb paid many learned Muslim men to write the
Fatawa-i Alamgiri over the course of eight years, from 1667
until 1675. The ulama also served as public censors under
Aurangzeb and as collectors of the jizya tax. Beginning in 1679
Aurangzeb levied the jizya on most non-Muslims in the empire
in lieu of military service (Rajput and Maratha state officials
and Brahmin religious leaders were exempt, but lay Jains, Sikhs,
and other non-Muslims were obliged to pay). The jizya tax had
been abated for one hundred years in the Mughal kingdom, and
Aurangzeb revived it, perhaps in part, to employ the ulama in

its collection. In theory, the jizya also helped Aurangzeb's reputation among the ulama, especially those suspicious of the religious sincerity of kings, by marking the Mughal Empire as a
proper Islamic state.

Many of Aurangzeb's nobles, including prominent Muslims
and royal family members such as Jahanara, Aurangzeb's eldest
sister, lampooned the jizya as a poor administrative decision. The
tax also upset many Hindus. A scathing letter to Aurangzeb,
perhaps penned by Shivaji or Rana Raj Singh, the Rajput ruler
of Mewar from 1652 to 1680, disparaged the jizya on the grounds
that it went against the notion of *sulh-i kull* (peace for all), which
had been a bedrock of Mughal policy since Akbar's time.

In practice, reinstating the jizya did not give Aurangzeb increased control over the powerful ulama. Numerous contemporaries railed against abuses in the jizya's collection, to the extent
that a huge percentage of jizya money never found its way past
the pockets of greedy tax collectors. Aurangzeb was impotent
to halt such theft.

Moral Policing

A king is a shepherd of the poor even if he cows them with his glory.
Sheep do not exist for the shepherd. It is the shepherd who exists for
serving the sheep.

—*Sa'di, Gulistan*

Aurangzeb's willingness to compromise his ideals notwithstanding, the king espoused a paternalistic view of his obligation
to his subjects. He considered himself responsible for ensuring
not only the physical but also the moral wellbeing of those living under his regime. Accordingly, he strove to encourage and
even coerce those within his kingdom to lead, in his estimation,
ethical lives.

Aurangzeb drew on Islamic ideas of justice and morality in projecting himself as a moral leader. His paternalistic tendencies were also likely molded by the dismal view of kings found in Persian ethical treatises such as Sa'di's *Gulistan* (Rose garden), which admonishes emperors to rule well but assumes most are vicious tyrants. Notably, Aurangzeb regulated the activities of Hindus and Muslims alike. In many cases he prescribed similar behaviors for his subjects regardless of religion. In other instances he addressed issues specific to one religious group, although he typically applied analogous principles to all.

Bans and restrictions numbered among the most common types of state policies that Aurangzeb used to promote morality among those living in Mughal India. At different points in his reign Aurangzeb tried to limit or bar the following vices: alcohol, opium, prostitution, gambling, inflammatory theological writings, and public celebrations of religious festivals. Censors (*muhtasibs*) were charged with enforcing moral codes, and each city had its own drawn from the ranks of the ulama. The justification and goal of such restrictions were the same: public and individual ethics. Basic concerns with state security also motivated some provisions, which then became tools for making Mughal India, in theory, an ethical and secure kingdom. For Aurangzeb, morality fell well within state authority and the broader duties of a king to safeguard the welfare of those he ruled.

·   ·   ·

Aurangzeb's attempt to reduce the consumption of alcohol across his empire was one of the more spectacular policy failures of his reign. Alcohol was widely condemned as un-Islamic, and Mughal kings had long been lauded across religious lines for encouraging temperance. For example, the Jain monk Shanticandra wrote around 1590 about how Akbar "banned liquor, which ought to be universally reviled." Jahangir also claimed to have proscribed alcohol (despite being a prolific drinker himself). The repeated appearance of this ban signals that it was ineffective.

In spite of the odds, Aurangzeb followed his forefathers and attempted to restrict the sale of wine and liquor. According to the testimony of the French traveler Francois Bernier, wine was "prohibited equally by the Gentile and Mahometan [Hindu and Muslim] law" and was hard to come by in Delhi. More generally, however, imbibing alcohol was rampant in Aurangzeb's India. William Norris, an English ambassador to Aurangzeb's court in the early eighteenth century, testified that Asad Khan (chief vizier from 1676 to 1707) and other government ministers were "fond of nothing more than hot spirits with which they make themselves drunk every day if they can get it." Accordingly, Norris tried to influence Asad Khan by sending him some liquor and choice glasses with which to imbibe the "strong waters."

While he personally declined to consume alcohol, Aurangzeb knew that few of his imperial officers followed his example. Niccoli Manucci—unleashing his characteristic weakness for gossip and exaggeration—wrote that Aurangzeb once exclaimed in exasperation that only two men in all of Hindustan did not drink: himself and his head qazi, Abdul Wahhab. Manucci, however, divulged to his readers: "But with respect to 'Abd-ul-wahhab [Aurangzeb] was in error, for I myself sent him every day a bottle of spirits (*vino*), which he drank in secret, so that the king could not find it out."

Aurangzeb's other attempts at censorship, such as curbing the production and use of opium, met with similarly dismal results.

. . .

Aurangzeb limited public observances of many religious holidays. These restrictions affected people of all religions, both be-

cause Aurangzeb regulated festivals belonging to all major religious groups in his empire and because Indians of the time, like
many Indians today, often celebrated one another's holy days.

In the eighth year of his reign Aurangzeb constrained ro-
bust festivities on Nauruz, the Persian New Year, and the major
Muslim holidays of Eid al-Fitr and Eid al-Adha, cancelling
"celebrations on a grand scale." Around the same time, he also
attempted to curb the revelry associated with the Hindu festivals of Holi and Diwali and the Muslim commemoration of
Muharram. Aurangzeb issued these commands, in part, because
he found the exuberance of revelers distasteful. But concerns
with public safety also lurked in the background of these orders.

Religious festivals were often hazardous affairs in medieval
India. For example, Bhimsen Saxena wrote about a large festival
held every twelve years near Trimbak, Maharashtra (possibly an
antecedent of the Kumbh Mela). Armed bands of ascetics gathered for the occasion and fought one another, resulting in significant fatalities. Jean de Thevenot, a French traveler to India,
reported that Muharram celebrations were so wild in Golconda
in 1666–67—with both Hindus and Muslims partaking—that
violence was standard. An incident in Burhanpur during the
1669 Muharram celebrations left more than fifty dead and one
hundred wounded. Theft and other crimes also marred religious
ceremonies in Mughal India, such as the penchant of Holi revelers in Gujarat to steal wood for making large fires. Aurangzeb
ordered his officials to crack down on this practice in the mid-
1660s along with the use of "obscene language" during both
Holi and Diwali.

Aurangzeb reduced carousing and illegal conduct at religious festivals, but he stopped short of banning such events altogether. In fact, early in his reign, Aurangzeb encouraged such

celebrations by rescinding taxes previously levied on Hindu festivals. Plentiful evidence suggests that people continued to par-
ticipate in public holiday observances throughout Aurangzeb's
rule. For example, numerous European travelers and Hindu
writers mentioned Holi celebrations as late as the 1690s. Even
Aurangzeb's own children celebrated non-Muslim religious festivals. In a letter from late in his life, Aurangzeb chastised his
son Muazzam for participating in Nauruz, an ancient Persian
festival that the king also identified as marking the coronation
day of Vikramaditya, a legendary Hindu ruler.

.   .   .

As part of his agenda to promote moral behavior, Aurangzeb
attempted to mold the theological leanings of his subjects, especially Muslims. Aurangzeb has received more press in recent
years for his alleged agenda to gain converts for Islam. In fact,
Aurangzeb's government never spearheaded a program to mar-
shal the widespread conversion of Hindus (or anybody else).
But some individuals found compelling reasons to adopt Islam.

Conversion to Islam could help individuals climb the Mughal hierarchy and made people eligible for jobs reserved for
Muslims, such as collectors of the jizya tax. But conversion also
brought men within the purview of Aurangzeb's scrutiny. In a
1699 letter, for example, Aurangzeb condemned two men who
"boasted much of their conversion to Islam" and spoke against
the emperor, labeling them "irreligious persons" (*bi-dinyan*). The
king ordered both imprisoned for their insincerity.

Overall, relatively few Hindus converted to Islam in Aurangzeb's India. This is made clear by regular news bulletins that arrived at the royal court reporting small-scale conversions, often
of low-level state employees, sometimes complete with the
names of the individuals involved.

Aurangzeb acted more proactively regarding Muslim subjects, however, and tried to affect their religious ideas at times, such as in his censorship of select writings of Ahmad Sirhindi (d. 1624). Ahmad Sirhindi, a member of the Sufi Naqshbandi order, was notorious for his polemicist views that incited controversy between Muslim communities. Although Sirhindi died toward the end of Jahangir's reign, his popularity spread during Shah Jahan's rule. His work was included in some madrasa curriculums, and many increasingly saw him as a renewer (*mujaddid*) of Islam, perhaps even a prophet. The Mughal Empire lacked a formal apparatus for censoring books in line with the efforts of contemporary European powers. But Aurangzeb singled out Sirhindi in the 1680s and banned certain of his theologically questionable writings.

At times, Aurangzeb persecuted specific Muslim groups whose doctrines ran afoul of his vision of Islam. In the 1640s, for example, when Aurangzeb was still a prince administering Gujarat, Mughal troops from Ahmedabad massacred a few dozen members of the Mahdavi, a Muslim millennial community founded in India in the late fifteenth century. The Mahdavis had political ambitions, which perhaps partly explains this strong response. Forty years later, when the Mahdavis had tempered both their political and religious stances, a Mahdavi delegation to the imperial court convinced Aurangzeb and his chief qazi that the group comprised harmless, mainstream Muslims.

Aurangzeb also went after nonpolitical Muslim communities deemed aberrant. Again during his princely years he targeted the Ismaili Bohras, a Shia community, and even executed one of their leaders. Aurangzeb harassed the Ismaili Bohras throughout his reign. For example, in his eighth year of rule he ordered Bohra mosques to hold five prayers daily in the Sunni style, and even decades later imperial soldiers periodically arrested members of this community.

.   .   .

Like earlier Mughal rulers, Aurangzeb drew a careful line between what was permissible to regulate in the name of public welfare versus what was a matter of individual taste. Music, for example, fell into the latter category. Aurangzeb is commonly thought to have banned music throughout his empire, a misunderstanding that scholars such as Katherine Schofield have corrected but has yet to filter into popular awareness (Aurangzeb only limited certain types of music within his own court).

Perhaps more interestingly, Aurangzeb did not prohibit satirical poetry, a popular genre at the time. One anecdote features a poet who wrote a coarse satire about the late-life second marriage of Kamgar Khan, a state official. The offended Kamgar Khan requested the king's intervention. Aurangzeb responded that the same poet "had not spared me [in his satires]; in return, I had increased his reward, that he might not do it again; yet in spite of this [favour] he had not on his part been less [satirical]." Aurangzeb then dismissed the petition, advising Kamgar Khan, whose ego had been bruised, "We ought to repress our feelings and live in harmony."

CHAPTER 6

Overseer of Hindu Religious Communities

Protector of Temples

[Ellora] is one of the finely crafted marvels of the real, transcendent
Artisan [i.e., God].

—*Aurangzeb describing the Hindu, Jain, and Buddhist temples at Ellora*

Hindu and Jain temples dotted the landscape of Aurangzeb's
kingdom. These religious institutions were entitled to Mughal
state protection, and Aurangzeb generally endeavored to ensure
their well-being. By the same token, from a Mughal perspective, that goodwill could be revoked when specific temples or
their associates acted against imperial interests. Accordingly,
Emperor Aurangzeb authorized targeted temple destructions
and desecrations throughout his rule.

Many modern people view Aurangzeb's orders to harm
specific temples as symptomatic of a larger vendetta against
Hindus. Such views have roots in colonial-era scholarship,
where positing timeless Hindu-Muslim animosity embodied
the British strategy of divide and conquer. Today, multiple web-
sites claim to list Aurangzeb's "atrocities" against Hindus (typically playing fast and loose with the facts) and fuel communal
fires. There are numerous gaping holes in the proposition that
Aurangzeb razed temples because he hated Hindus, however.
Most glaringly, Aurangzeb counted thousands of Hindu temples within his domains and yet destroyed, at most, a few dozen.
This incongruity makes little sense if we cling to a vision of

Aurangzeb as a cartoon bigot driven by a single-minded agenda of ridding India of Hindu places of worship. A historically legitimate view of Aurangzeb must explain why he protected Hindu temples more often than he demolished them.

Aurangzeb followed Islamic law in granting protections to non-Muslim religious leaders and institutions. Indo-Muslim rulers had counted Hindus within the Islamic juridical category of *dhimmi*s since the eighth century, and Hindus were thus entitled to certain rights and state defenses. Yet Aurangzeb went beyond the requirements of Islamic law in his conduct toward Hindu and Jain religious communities. Instead, for Aurangzeb, protecting and, at times, razing temples served the cause of ensuring justice for all throughout the Mughal Empire.

Aurangzeb's notion of justice included a certain measure of freedom of religion, which led him to protect most places of Hindu worship. Mughal rulers in general allowed their subjects great leeway—shockingly so compared to the draconian measures instituted by many European sovereigns of the era—to follow their own religious ideas and inclinations. Nonetheless, state interests constrained religious freedom in Mughal India, and Aurangzeb did not hesitate to strike hard against religious institutions and leaders that he deemed seditious or immoral. But absent such concerns, Aurangzeb's vision of himself as an even-handed ruler of all Indians prompted him to extend state security to temples.

. . .

Aurangzeb laid out his vision of how good kings ought to treat temples and other non-Muslim religious sites in a princely order (*nishan* in Persian) that he sent to Rana Raj Singh, the Hindu Rajput ruler of Mewar, in 1654: "Because the persons of great kings are shadows of God, the attention of this elevated class, who are the pillars of God's court, is devoted to this: that men of various dispositions and different religions (*mazahib*) should live in the vale of peace and pass their days in prosperity, and no one should meddle in the affairs of another." When we strip away the flowery style of formal Persian, Aurangzeb's point is this: kings represent God on earth and are thus obliged to ensure peace among religious communities.

In the same princely order Aurangzeb condemned any king "who resorted to bigotry (*taassub*)" as guilty of "razing God's prosperous creations and destroying divine foundations." Aurangzeb promised to turn his back on such un-Islamic practices once he ascended the throne and instead to "cast luster on the four-cornered, inhabited world" by following "the revered practices and established regulations" of his "great ancestors." In Aurangzeb's eyes Islamic teachings and the Mughal tradition enjoined him to protect Hindu temples, pilgrimage destinations, and holy men.

Aurangzeb had forty-nine years to make good on his princely promise of cultivating religious tolerance in the Mughal Empire, and he got off to a strong start. In one of his early acts as emperor, Aurangzeb issued an imperial order (*farman*) to local Mughal officials at Benares that directed them to halt any interference in the affairs of local temples. Writing in February of 1659, Aurangzeb said he had learned that "several people have, out of spite and rancour, harassed the Hindu residents of Banaras and nearby places, including a group of Brahmins who are in charge of ancient temples there." The king then ordered his officials: "You must see that nobody unlawfully disturbs the Brahmins or other Hindus of that region, so that they might remain in their traditional place and pray for the continuance of the Empire."

The ending of the 1659 Benares *farman* became a common refrain in the many imperial commands penned by Aurangzeb that protected temples and their caretakers: they should be left alone so that Brahmins could pray for the longevity of the Mughal state.

.   .   .

Throughout his reign Aurangzeb's default policy was to ensure the well-being of Hindu religious institutions and their leaders. He issued dozens of orders that directed officials to shield temples from unwanted interference, granted land to Hindu communities, and provided stipends to Hindu spiritual figures.

For instance, in the ninth year of his reign Aurangzeb dispensed a *farman* to the Umanand Temple at Gauhati in Assam confirming an earlier land grant and the associated right to collect revenue. In 1680 he directed that Bhagwant Gosain, a Hindu ascetic who lived on the banks of the Ganges in Benares, should be kept free from harassment. In 1687 the emperor gave some empty land on a ghat in Benares (which was, incidentally, near a mosque) to Ramjivan Gosain in order to build houses for "pious Brahmins and holy faqirs." In 1691 Aurangzeb conferred eight villages and a sizable chunk of tax-free land on Mahant Balak Das Nirvani of Chitrakoot to support the Balaji Temple. In 1698 he gifted rent-free land to a Brahmin named Rang Bhatt, son of Nek Bhatt, in eastern Khandesh in central India. The list goes on and includes temples and individuals in Allahabad, Vrindavan, Bihar, and elsewhere.

Aurangzeb carried on the traditions of his forefathers in granting favors to Hindu religious communities, a continuity underscored by his dealings with the Jangam. The Jangam, a Shaivite group, benefited from Mughal orders beginning under Akbar, who confirmed their legal rights to land in 1564. The

same Jangam received several *farmans* from Aurangzeb that re-
stored land that had been unfairly confiscated (1667), protected
them from a disruptive local Muslim (1672), and returned ille-
gally charged rent (1674). Such measures ensured that pious individuals could continue their religious activities, a component
of Aurangzeb's vision of justice.

Aurangzeb enacted similarly favorable policies toward
Jain religious institutions. Again following Akbar's example,
Aurangzeb granted land at Shatrunjaya, Girnar, and Mount
Abu—all Jain pilgrimage destinations in Gujarat—to specific
Jain communities in the late 1650s. He gave Lal Vijay, a Jain
monk, a monastery (*poshala*), probably sometime before 1681,
and granted relief for a resting house (*upashraya*) in 1679. As
late as 1703, Aurangzeb issued orders prohibiting people from
harassing Jina Chandra Suri, a Jain religious leader. Given such
actions, it is unsurprising that we find laudatory descriptions
of the emperor in vernacular Jain works of this period, such as,
"Aurangzeb Shah is a brave and powerful king" (*mardano aur
mahabali aurangasahi naranda*).

.   .   .

In 1672 Aurangzeb issued an order recalling all endowed lands
given to Hindus and reserving all such future land grants for
Muslims, possibly as a concession to the ulama. If strictly en-
forced, this move would have been a significant blow to Hindu
and Jain religious communities, but historical evidence suggests
otherwise.

The new policy on land grants lacked implementation,
especially in more far-flung areas of the kingdom. In parts of
Bengal, for instance, Mughal officers gave more endowed land
to Hindus after the 1672 order than before. Abundant individual cases also signal that the recall was more in theory than

practice. In Gujarat, for example, a family of Parsi physicians received confirmation of a prior land grant in 1702, toward the end of Aurangzeb's reign. Likewise, several of the examples I cited above from other regions indicate the limited reach of this policy. Based on the evidence, some modern historians have suggested that the 1672 order was followed almost nowhere in the empire, remaining "on paper only" except in select areas such as the Punjab.

There were other moments when Aurangzeb showed anxiety concerning Hindu temples. In the 1659 Benares order that I discuss above, for example, Aurangzeb noted that Islamic law (*shariat*) mandated that "ancient temples should not be torn down" but then added "nor should new temples be built." This restriction was specific to Benares, as Richard Eaton has pointed out, and plenty of Hindu temples were built elsewhere in Mughal India during Aurangzeb's reign. Still, the command was an abrupt departure from earlier Mughal policy that suggests the complexity—and the limits—of Aurangzeb's protection of Hindu temples.

Destroyer of Temples

It is not lawful to lay waste ancient idol temples, and it does not rest with you to prohibit ablution in a reservoir which has been customary from ancient times.

> —*Advice given by Muslim jurists to the future Sikander Lodi of Delhi*
> *(r. 1489–1517)*

Of the tens of thousands of Hindu and Jain temples located within Mughal domains, most, although not all, still stood at the end of Aurangzeb's reign.

Nobody knows the exact number of temples demolished or pillaged on Aurangzeb's orders, and we never will. Richard

Eaton, the leading authority on the subject, puts the number of confirmed temple destructions during Aurangzeb's rule at just over a dozen, with fewer tied to the emperor's direct commands. Other scholars have pointed out additional temple demolitions not counted by Eaton, such as two orders to destroy the Somanatha Temple in 1659 and 1706 (the existence of a second order suggests that the first was never carried out). Aurangzeb also oversaw temple desecrations. For example, in 1645 he ordered *mihrab*s (prayer niches, typically located in mosques) erected in Ahmedabad's Chintamani Parshvanath Temple, built by the Jain merchant Shantidas. Even adding in such events, however, to quote Eaton, "the evidence is almost always fragmentary, incomplete, or even contradictory." Given this, there were probably more temples destroyed under Aurangzeb than we can confirm (perhaps a few dozen in total?), but here we run into a dark curtain drawn across an unknown past.

A few beams of suggestive light shine through, however, that suggest temple destructions were relatively infrequent in Aurangzeb's India. For example, the *Maasir-i Alamgiri* of Saqi Mustaid Khan, a Persian-language chronicle written shortly after Aurangzeb's death, characterized the 1670 destruction of Mathura's Keshava Deva Temple as "a rare and impossible event that came into being seemingly from nowhere." The *Maasir-i Alamgiri* overall presented Aurangzeb's reign through the lens of Islamic conquest, sometimes changing facts to suit the author's tastes. This tendency means that the work—as much a rhetorical masterpiece as a history—must be cited with extreme caution. The *Maasir-i Alamgiri* has a noted tendency to exaggerate the number of temples demolished by Aurangzeb, which adds credence to its acknowledgment here that such events were unusual and unexpected.

In the case of precolonial temple destruction in India, it is a fool's errand to get "swept up in a numbers game," as Eaton has put it. We stand on firmer ground in reconstructing the reasons that prompted Aurangzeb to target specific Hindu temples while leaving the vast majority untouched.

. . .

Political events incited Aurangzeb to initiate assaults on certain Hindu temples. For example, Aurangzeb ordered Benares's Vishvanatha Temple demolished in 1669 and Mathura's Keshava Deva Temple brought down in 1670. In both instances Aurangzeb sought to punish political missteps by temple associates and ensure future submission to the Mughal state.

The idea that religious institutions could be subject to politically motivated destructions makes many modern people see red, but premodern Indians did not draw such a firm line between religion and politics. On the contrary, temples were widely understood—by both Hindus and Muslims—as linked with political action. The Sanskrit *Brihatsamhita*, written perhaps in the sixth century, warns, "If a Shiva linga, image, or temple breaks apart, moves, sweats, cries, speaks, or otherwise acts with no apparent cause, this warns of the destruction of the king and his territory." Acting on this premise that religious images held political power, Hindu kings targeted one another's temples beginning in the seventh century, regularly looting and defiling images of Durga, Ganesha, Vishnu, and so forth. They also periodically destroyed each other's temples. Some Hindu kings even commissioned Sanskrit poetry to celebrate and memorialize such actions. Indo-Muslim rulers, such as Aurangzeb, followed suit in considering Hindu temples legitimate targets of punitive state action.

Aurangzeb brought the bulk of Benares's Vishvanatha Temple down in 1669. The temple had been built during Akbar's reign by Raja Man Singh, whose great-grandson, Jai Singh, many believed helped Shivaji flee from the Mughal court in 1666 (following Jai Singh's earlier military assault on Shivaji). Additionally, in 1669 a rebellion broke out among Benares landlords connected to the Vishvanatha Temple, many of whom were also implicated in Shivaji's escape.

In 1670 Aurangzeb directed the obliteration of the Keshava Deva Temple in Mathura, built in 1618 by Bir Singh Bundela, for similarly layered political reasons. Mathura Brahmins may have assisted with Shivaji's 1666 flight from Agra. Moreover, the Keshava Deva Temple had been patronized by Dara Shukoh, Aurangzeb's major rival for the throne. More immediately, Jat uprisings in the region in 1669 and 1670 dealt the Mughals heavy casualties. In subsequent years Aurangzeb ordered temples demolished in Jodhpur, Khandela, and elsewhere for similar reasons.

Mosques were erected on the former sites of both the Vishvanatha and Keshava Deva Temples, although they were built under different circumstances. The Gyanvapi Masjid still stands today in Benares with part of the ruined temple's wall incorporated into the building. This reuse may have been a religiously clothed statement about the dire consequences of opposing Mughal authority. Convenience may also have dictated this recycling. While the Gyanvapi Mosque dates to Aurangzeb's period, its patron is unknown, and the structure is not mentioned in Mughal documents.

Aurangzeb sponsored the mosque that replaced Mathura's Keshava Deva Temple. This may be explained by the death of Abdul Nabi Khan, a Mughal commander and a patron of the major mosque in Mathura, during the Jat rebellion. A mere eight months after Abdul Nabi's death, a loss within the patronage community of Mathura mosques, the Keshava Deva Temple lay in ruins.

.   .   .

While we can reconstruct the politics of Mughal temple destruction, medieval observers rarely, if ever, outlined realpolitik arguments for attacking specific sites. Many Hindu and Jain thinkers chalked up temple demolitions to the degeneracy of the Kali Yuga, the current age. Muslim writers commonly fell back on jihad or some other religious-based concept in their narrations of temple destructions. This Islamic proclivity was perhaps rooted in the idea that government interests do not justify harming religious institutions under Islamic law, whereas such acts were arguably permissible for spreading Islam. This logic was culturally appropriate, but it is not historically persuasive for explaining temple demolitions in Aurangzeb's India.

Although the Kali Yuga and jihad fail to explain—in historical terms—why Aurangzeb razed certain temples while leaving most unmolested, alternative religious reasons may well have been at play. According to Saqi Mustaid Khan, a historian who wrote after Aurangzeb's death, in 1669 the king learned that "in Thatta, Multan, and especially at Benares, deviant Brahmins were teaching false books at their established schools. Curious seekers—Hindu and Muslim alike—traveled great distances to gain depraved knowledge from them." Similar issues may have been present in the case of Mathura's Keshava Deva Temple, which attracted Muslims as early as Jahangir's reign.

Generations of Mughal kings had attempted to curb certain religious behaviors, especially those of errant Brahmins who, in Mughal eyes, took advantage of the less sophisticated. For example, Akbar took Brahmins to task for misrepresenting Hindu texts to lower castes and hoped that translating Sanskrit texts into Persian would prompt these (in his opinion) arrogant leaders to reform their ways.

Aurangzeb similarly evinced concern with elite Brahmins deceiving common Hindus about their own religion and was perhaps especially alarmed that Muslims were falling prey to charlatans. Brahmins may even have profited financially from such ventures. The French traveler Jean de Thevenot opined that Brahmins were numerous in Benares and "find their Profit" in lavish festivals that drew large crowds. In such cases Mughal royal obligations demanded strong intervention to prevent their subjects from being hoodwinked. For most temples in Benares and elsewhere, Aurangzeb ordered Mughal officials to investigate alleged dubious practices. But in the case of certain institutions, including the Vishvanatha and Keshava Deva Temples, he deemed demolition appropriate.

.   .   .

Most of the temples that Aurangzeb targeted were in northern India. With only a handful of exceptions, Aurangzeb did not destroy temples in the Deccan, where he and his vast army expanded the Mughal kingdom during the last three decades of his life. There were plentiful temples to be demolished in central and southern India, and the Mughals threw their military might against forts and other military targets in these regions. But Aurangzeb did not consider temple demolition consistent with successfully incorporating new areas within the Mughal Empire.

Even when Aurangzeb faced significant opposition in expanding Mughal rule southward, he used other tactics to solicit compliance. This approach suggests, among other things, that Aurangzeb and his officers understood that temple destruction was an extreme measure and so used it sparingly.

CHAPTER 7

Later Years

Conqueror of the Deccan

I have found the men of the world very greedy, so much so that an emperor like Aurangzeb Alamgir, who wants for nothing, has been seized with such a longing and passion for taking forts that he personally runs about panting for some heaps of stone.

—*Persian memoir of Bhimsen Saxena, a Hindu soldier, 1707*

If a man of God eats half a loaf, he will give the other half to the poor.
A king can seize the territory of a whole clime, but he will still crave another.

—*Sa'di, Gulistan*

Aurangzeb left behind the Peacock Throne of Delhi and moved to the Deccan in the early 1680s. He had run through commander after commander of Mughal expansion campaigns in the Deccan, and all had fallen short. The Mughals had coveted the Deccan since Akbar's time and launched numerous military assaults within the region over the previous century. But Aurangzeb devoted unprecedented resources to conquering south India by living out his final decades on the battlefield.

Aurangzeb marched south with an entourage of tens of thousands, including all of his living sons (except Prince Akbar, who was in rebellion) and his harem. The mobile, tented camp was surely a site to behold with its traveling bazaar, army, and bewildering array of bureaucratic officers and servants. After many months the caravan reached the Deccan, and Aurangzeb set his sights on conquest.

Mughal kings were often peripatetic, and Aurangzeb followed a grand Mughal tradition that the capital moved with the
king. Still, Aurangzeb was innovative in permanently relocating
south. Delhi appeared to many a ghost town in his absence and
lost a significant portion of its population. The rooms of the
Red Fort grew dusty, unfit to be viewed by visiting dignitaries.

In terms of territorial expansion, Aurangzeb enjoyed unpar-
alleled success in his Deccan ventures. He used both military
and diplomatic resources to expand Mughal control across the
southern half of the subcontinent. But, even while Aurangzeb
lived, signs cropped up that the Deccan wars boded ill for the
future of the Mughal state. Aurangzeb's later decades of ruth-
less assaults and endless sieges were superficially successful but,
ultimately, hollow.

.   .   .

Among Aurangzeb's many Deccan victories, the sultanates of
Bijapur and Golconda stand out as crucial, if costly, conquests.

In 1685 Aurangzeb besieged Bijapur, which had been under
the rule of the Adil Shahis since 1489, with an army of eighty
thousand men. Bijapur's ruler, Sikandar, and thirty thousand
men were trapped inside the city's fortified walls for more than
fifteen months. Many starved to death on both sides, but the
Mughals held out until Sikandar Adil Shah capitulated. The
defeated ruler came before Aurangzeb in 1686 and bowed low
to the ground to signal his acceptance of Mughal sovereignty.

Golconda, controlled by the Qutb Shahi dynasty and first
established around 1518, fell to Mughal forces in 1687 owing to
an act of treachery. The Mughals first drove much of the Qutb
Shahi army into Golconda Fort and then created a blockade
(fig. 6). The Mughal army waited patiently for eight months
while they starved the Qutb Shahi forces of food, water, and

Figure 6. Emperor Aurangzeb at the Siege of Golconda in 1687, c. 1750–90. Anne S. K. Brown Military Collection, Brown University Library.

reinforcements. Unable to bear such deprivation any longer, a lone official accepted a bribe from Aurangzeb to leave a fort gate ajar one night. Mughal troops swept in and took the fort in hours, thereby subsuming the Qutb Shahi kingdom and its famed diamond mines within the Mughal umbrella.

After Golconda, the Marathas were the major remaining opponents of Aurangzeb. Maratha leaders lost Jinji (Gingee), a fort in Tamil Nadu, to the Mughals in 1698. Between 1699 and 1706 Aurangzeb's forces assaulted one dozen hill forts held by Marathas, and Mughal borders swelled, coming ever closer to encompassing the entire subcontinent. In total, Aurangzeb added four new Mughal provinces, which collectively made up more than one-quarter of the entire Mughal kingdom. But these land acquisitions were short-lived. Within a few decades of Aurangzeb's death the Mughals lost all that he had gained in the Deccan, and the empire began to crumble.

.   .   .

Even during Aurangzeb's life, military strikes in the Deccan raised hefty problems for the Mughal state. The constant warring depleted the treasury and sapped the will of many nobles. Especially Rajputs and other North Indians were ill-content to toil for decades in southern India, far from home and subjected to a climate, culture, and people that they did not consider their own. For instance, Bhimsen Saxena, a Kayasth from Uttar Pradesh whose family had served the Mughals for generations, wrote frankly about the hardships of travel and long separations from family. He characterized South Indians as an utterly foreign people who disgusted him. Describing the Deccan battles of the mid-1690s, Bhimsen wrote about southern Hindus: "They are dark of complexion, ill-shaped and ugly of form. If a man who has not seen them before, encounters them

in the dark night, he will most likely die of fright." Faced with
life among people that they viewed as repulsive, many felt that
Mughal service had lost its appeal.

For other imperial officials, life in the South proved tol-
erable, but the Mughal *mansab* system creaked under its own
weight. Nobles often had to wait years to receive land from
which they could collect income (*jagir*s). In the meantime they
lacked resources to pay the soldiers that the Mughal state expected them to employ. Disloyalty and disregarding orders were
commonplace.

The siege of Jinji offers some indication of the unrest that
overtook many Mughal troops and nobles during the Deccan
years. Aurangzeb occupied Jinji in 1698 but only after an eight-
year siege. The length of this protracted siege is hard to justify,
and observers at the time typically blamed the commander, Zulfiqar Khan, for being unwilling to commit to the task. Rumors
flew about, including that Zulfiqar Khan was in cahoots with
the Marathas who controlled Jinji and that he wanted to avoid
being dispatched to desolate Qandahar, a plausible next posting.
In any case, unnecessarily prolonging a siege suggests that army
morale and imperial authority were slipping.

.   .   .

While his men wavered, Aurangzeb's drive to conquer accelerated as he aged. In addition to spending his sixties, sev-
enties, and eighties in the Deccan, the king often personally
oversaw battles and sieges. As Bhimsen put it, none too kindly,
"[Aurangzeb] runs about panting for some heaps of stone."
Aurangzeb thrived on his increased activity, ordering marches
to continue whether he was well or ill. He wrote to an administrator, "So long as a single breath of this mortal life remains,
there is no release from labour and work." Unlike many of his

officers, the king also enjoyed living in the South. Back in his princely days he had written to his father praising the Deccan's fresh air, sweet water, and extensive cultivation.

Many of Aurangzeb's activities in the South bore a high cost in terms of human life and livelihood. The Mughals and Marathas alike scorched the countryside, and famines swept certain areas. Mughal sieges sometimes decimated populations, as did the diseases that followed. For example, in 1690 Bijapur's population was half of what it had been a mere five years earlier, before the Mughal assault and a subsequent cholera epidemic. Cries for mercy did not compel Aurangzeb to abandon his push for expansion or adjust his tactics, although he periodically granted small measures of relief. For example, he gave tax breaks to hard-hit regions, cancelling the jizya for Hyderabad in 1688–89 because of drought and remitting the jizya for the entire Deccan in 1704 in consideration of the toll of famines and war. Such measures likely did little to mitigate the hardships foisted on many by Mughal and Maratha clashes.

Aurangzeb was an emperor, and as such he needed no special justification for seeking to enlarge his empire. But still, one wonders what drove such aggressive ventures into his old age and against the better judgment of many Mughal officers. Was Aurangzeb frustrated by the persistence of Maratha fighters, who were no match for the Mughals in open battle but often effectively used speed, surprise, and guerilla tactics against imperial troops? Did Aurangzeb believe that more territory would shore up the Mughal state? Did he devote so much of his life to conquering southern India that he did not know how to quit? Whatever his reasons, it seems that Aurangzeb lost himself in the drive to acquire more and more territory.

Dying King

Too great is the grief of this world, and I have only one heart bud—
how can I pour all the desert's sand into an hourglass?

—*Aurangzeb*

Aurangzeb's final years were largely filled with war, but the king also found time to reflect on his life and the future of the Mughal state. As the king rode (and, increasingly, was carried) around the Deccan (fig. 7), he wrote letters to generals, imperial officials, and family members. These documents capture his insights and regrets about his life, his place in Indian history, and the great experiment of the Mughal Empire.

Some of Aurangzeb's concerns in his old age were mundane and utterly human. For instance, he wrote repeatedly about mangoes, one of his favorite fruits. The Mughal love of the mango dated back to Babur, the founder of the Mughal Empire, who wrote in his memoirs, "When the mango is good it is *really* good." Aurangzeb requested his sons and imperial officials to send baskets of mangoes and was appreciative when they complied. Aurangzeb playfully named unfamiliar species with Hindi terms derived from Sanskrit vocabulary, like *sudharas* (ambrosia-nectared) and *rasnabilas* (tongue-pleasing). He grumbled when his mango shipments arrived spoiled.

Aurangzeb also reminisced about his younger years and perhaps happier days with his family. In a 1700 letter to Prince Azam, the king invoked a memory from his son's childhood when, imitating the royal drums and using a Hindi word for *father*, the prince had exclaimed, "Babaji, dhun, dhun." In his last years Aurangzeb especially enjoyed the company of Udaipuri, Kam Bakhsh's mother and, curiously, a musician. In a deathbed letter to Kam Bakhsh, Aurangzeb wrote that Udaipuri was with

Figure 7. The Emperor Aurangzeb Carried on a Palanquin. Painting by Bhavanidas,
c. 1705–20. Metropolitan Museum of Art, New York, Louis V. Bell Fund, 2003,
2003.430.

him in illness and would soon follow him in death. Udaipuri died in the summer of 1707, a few months after Aurangzeb.

As often as he looked back, however, Aurangzeb looked forward in his final years, and he disliked what he saw.

.   .   .

Aurangzeb feared for the future of his kingdom, and he had good reason to do so. In addition to the plethora of financial and administrative problems that beleaguered the Mughal state, Aurangzeb saw nobody on the horizon capable of navigating such difficulties.

Aurangzeb had three surviving sons at the time of his death (two others had predeceased their father), none of whom he considered kingly material. In an early eighteenth-century letter, for example, Aurangzeb lashed out at his second son, Muazzam, for failing to take Qandahar, chastising him with the bitter saying, "A daughter is better than an unworthy son." He ended the letter by pointedly asking Muazzam, "How will you show your face to your rivals in this world and to the Holy, High, and Exalted God in the next?"

Aurangzeb did not recognize that he bore the brunt of responsibility for his sons' being ill-prepared to ascend the Mughal throne. Munis Faruqui has written eloquently about how Aurangzeb shackled Mughal princes by interfering in princely households and undercutting princely autonomy. By the 1700s Aurangzeb favored his grandsons over his sons, which further weakened the positions of the latter. Aurangzeb even privileged nobles above princes at times, such as when his chief vizier Asad Khan and military commander Zulfiqar Khan arrested Kam Bakhsh, Aurangzeb's youngest son, with impunity in 1693 after Kam Bakhsh had opened illicit negotiations with the Maratha

ruler Rajaram at Jinji. In Aurangzeb's purported last will he
partitioned the Mughal Empire among his three sons and appointed specific officials, including Asad Khan, in perpetuity.

Generations of Mughal princes had built extensive net-
works that brought new groups into the Mughal fold and en-
abled the princes to fight for the crown of an undivided empire. In short, succession struggles renewed and enlivened the
Mughal state. Aurangzeb declawed Mughal princes, however,
leaving them unable to fight or rule when the moment came.

                              ·   ·   ·

While blind to how restricting his sons harmed the Mughal
state, Aurangzeb grasped other crucial aspects of Mughal kingship. Aurangzeb's later letters to his sons and grandsons capture
his capacious vision of Mughal sovereignty.

In a post-1691 letter to his grandson Bidar Bakht, the eldest son of Azam Shah, Aurangzeb proffered advice about how
to best live and rule. He opened by recommending morning
prayer and Quranic recitation over water, which should then
be drunk, to counter disease and danger. He next advised Bidar
Bakht to adopt the old Mughal ritual, dating back to Akbar's
reign, of weighing oneself against various items and distribut-
ing the goods to the needy. Aurangzeb recognized the Hindu
roots of this custom, writing, "Although weighing one's entire
body against gold, silver, copper, grain, oil, and other commodi-
ties is not a practice of our ancestral lands or of the Muslims
here [in India], nonetheless the practice greatly benefits many
needy and poor people." In his letter the king reported to his
grandson that Shah Jahan had weighed himself twice a year but
counseled Bidar Bakht to execute the ceremony fourteen times
annually. As we have seen, Aurangzeb performed the weighing
rites himself for the first decade of his rule but then retired the

practice (he may have revived it in later years, according to a
report by the chaplain John Ovington). Aurangzeb recognized
the Hindu-based weighing ritual as part of the Indian Mughal
tradition, even if he had personally shied away from it.

Similarly, in a late letter written to his son Azam Shah,
Aurangzeb endorsed Shah Jahan's enjoyment of music, something Aurangzeb had given up decades ago, as a proper kingly
activity. There were many ways to be a Mughal king. In his late
letters Aurangzeb endorsed the syncretism that was a part of
his bloodline as a great strength that might enable the empire
to survive in the face of formidable opposition.

· · ·

Aurangzeb died of natural causes in early 1707 at Ahmed-
nagar in central India. As per his wishes he was interred at
an unmarked grave located within the Chishti Sufi shrine of
Zaynuddin Shirazi (d. 1369) in Khuldabad. You can visit his
grave today, although there is not much to see in the small,
open-air space. The shrine draws far fewer visitors annually than
the soaring mausoleums of Humayun, Akbar, and Shah Jahan.

Aurangzeb's simple grave is the antithesis of his complicated life. In its solemnity and setting, his burial choice was
meant to underscore his piety. Indeed, Aurangzeb grew increasingly concerned with religious matters toward the end of his
life, although in a different way than the king's modern detractors have imagined. Rather than behaving fanatically toward
others, Aurangzeb's devotion manifested itself in inward wor-
ries that he had acted against the will of God. He referred to
the Day of Judgment often in his later letters and wrote about
himself as a stranger about to enter the next world.

This multifaceted king had a complex relationship with
Islam, and even so he is not reducible to his religion. In fact,

little is simple about Aurangzeb. Aurangzeb was an emperor devoted to power, his vision of justice, and expansion. He was an administrator with streaks of brilliance and scores of faults. He grew the Mughal Empire to its greatest extent and may also have positioned it to break apart. No single characteristic or action can encapsulate Aurangzeb Alamgir, who adorned the Mughal throne for nearly fifty years and has captivated people's imaginations for far longer.

CHAPTER 8

Aurangzeb's Legacy

After Aurangzeb

None but the Creator has knowledge of the future;
If anyone says he knows it, do not believe him!

*—Baba Musafir (d. 1714), a Naqshbandi Sufi saint,
speaking about the war of succession among Aurangzeb's sons*

In the decades following Aurangzeb's death the Mughal Empire fragmented. Recent scholarship has suggested that post-Aurangzeb Mughal decline was not as swift or total as often presumed. But even allowing for great nuance, the downhill descent of the Mughal kingdom after Aurangzeb's death is striking.

The emperor's three surviving sons fought one another in a war of succession. In less than two years his second son, Muazzam, killed the other two, Azam and Kam Bakhsh, in battle and ascended the Mughal throne under the name Bahadur Shah. On the surface everything appeared to be business as usual. A succession struggle was expected and usually rejuvenated Mughal power. But instead, deep-rooted problems plagued this next phase of Mughal rule.

Bahadur Shah inherited from Aurangzeb several ongoing threats to the integrity of the Mughal state. Jats and Sikhs offered armed resistance in the North, the Maratha insurgency raged in the South, ineffective taxes left the royal coffers empty, and Rajputs rebelled. Many of these problems worsened upon Bahadur Shah's ascension as people seized the opportunity created by political transition to mount renewed challenges to Mughal authority. But, unlike his father, Bahadur Shah became overwhelmed by the opposition to Mughal sovereignty.

For example, the Rathor Rajput family of Marwar—who had unsuccessfully revolted against Aurangzeb thirty years earlier—tried, once again, to throw off Mughal control. The Rathor ruler, Ajit Singh, drove Mughal forces out of Jodhpur and even destroyed mosques erected during the imperial occupation of the city. Bahadur Shah retook Jodhpur. But soon Ajit Singh gained increased freedom for Marwar, largely because Bahadur Shah was distracted by a Sikh-led revolt in the Punjab, another lingering unrest from Aurangzeb's reign.

Bahadur Shah died in 1712, just five years after his father, and thereafter the Mughal Empire fractured at an accelerated rate. In the seven years between 1712 and 1719 four Mughal kings ruled in quick succession. In total five kings ascended the Mughal throne in the thirteen years after Aurangzeb's death, as compared to four kings in the previous one hundred and fifty years. In the face of such political instability the Mughal royal family lost sway over the nobility and found themselves unable to exercise even basic functions of kingship, such as consistent tax collection. Corruption ran rampant throughout the imperial administration, and many areas broke off from the Mughal state.

.   .   .

In 1739 the Iranian warlord Nadir Shah sacked Delhi, trampling on what remained of Mughal pride. He held the Mughal emperor Muhammad Shah hostage while Nadir Shah's troops slaughtered scores of Delhiites and looted the treasury of its immense wealth. When Nadir Shah returned to Iran two months later, among his plunders were some of the most prized symbols of Mughal sovereignty, including the Peacock Throne and the Kohinoor diamond.

A portrait of Nadir Shah was painted shortly after the invasion that showed him adorned with heavy jewelry, literally wearing the spoils of Mughal wealth. The Mughal kingdom never fully recovered after Nadir Shah's raid. As a Muslim intellectual of the day put it, the "sultanate of Delhi had become a child's game."

The Mughal Empire limped forward until the mid-nineteenth century, when it was brought to a formal end in a British court-room following the Sepoy Rebellion of 1857. But by that point it was an "empire" in name only. From the late 1750s onward, the East India Company stripped the already-reduced Mughals of nearly all the trappings of actual sovereigns, including their land-holdings, an army, and the ability to collect revenue. The penul-timate Mughal ruler, Akbar Shah II (r. 1806–37), was reduced to serving as a living museum exhibit and charged foreign visitors for an audience in order to make ends meet.

. . .

Scholars have reached no consensus on what caused the fall of Mughal power or even exactly when the Mughal state began to crack beyond repair. But most historians think that Aurangzeb was at least partly to blame. This is a curious argument because Aurangzeb expanded the Mughal state to its greatest extent geo-graphically. But perhaps Aurangzeb's success was also his ruin. He may have stretched the Mughal Empire too far, thus spread-ing imperial resources thin and making the entire apparatus prone to shattering.

More dubiously, some have proposed that Aurangzeb's al-leged austerity was a fatal flaw. For instance, Jadunath Sarkar, who did more scholarly work than anybody else in the twenti-eth century on Aurangzeb, put it thus in his dramatic style: "[in Aurangzeb's reign] the Mughal crescent rounded to fulness [*sic*] and then began to wane visibly." Jadunath Sarkar spelled out his vision of Aurangzeb in his many books on the man, including the five-volume *History of Aurangzib*. The final tome begins, "The life of Aurangzib was one long tragedy,—a story of man battling in vain against an invisible but inexorable Fate, a tale of how the strongest human endeavor was baffled by the forces of the age." For Sarkar, Aurangzeb was a tragic figure. Moreover, in line with other colonial-era thinkers, Sarkar viewed Aurangzeb as a religious zealot (hence, "the Mughal *crescent*") and thought that his dedication to a specific sort of Islam spelled utter catastrophe for the empire.

Few historians today take Sarkar's religious-based explanation of Mughal decline seriously, but it remains a popular view in the public eye. In part, this is a narrative—rather than a historical—problem. It appeals to a human desire for moralistic storytelling to identify an individual as responsible for toppling a powerful, wealthy state. Muslim villains are especially in vogue these days, which makes Aurangzeb the Pious an appealing scapegoat. In contrast, modern historians point to an array of social, fiscal, and administrative factors that weakened Mughal power. Such a diffuse, system-based explanation makes for better history but a pedestrian story line.

Frankly, we know too little about Mughal India post-Aurangzeb, and we also remain in the dark about many aspects of his reign that are pertinent to discerning his potential role in hollowing out the Mughal state. But Aurangzeb foresaw the possibility that he would leave a sour legacy. In his late letters he often worried about dark days ahead for the Mughal kingdom, even as he felt powerless to alter the empire's downward trajectory.

. . .

Aside from Aurangzeb's potential culpability in initiating the collapse of the Mughal Empire, how do we assess the long, uneven reign of this complex, sometimes contradictory, king? It offers little insight to condemn Aurangzeb according to modern standards concerning state violence, individual liberties, and tolerance. But we can more fruitfully ask how he compared to other rulers of his time, especially earlier Mughal emperors.

Aurangzeb broke from Mughal practices more than any prior Mughal king, at least since Akbar, who established many Mughal customs. Nonetheless, even accounting for changes such as reducing imperial patronage to certain arts, moving to the Deccan, and reintroducing the jizya tax, Aurangzeb exhibited overarching continuity with Mughal administrative, military, and cultural programs. He was not a cross-cultural pioneer on par with Akbar (perhaps, as the sixth ruler of an Indian empire, he did not feel the need to be). But Aurangzeb supported large-scale intellectual projects such as the *Fatawa-i Alamgiri* and was the dedicatee for multiple Persian *Ramayana*s. Aurangzeb was not a monumental builder the equal of Shah Jahan, although he was not far off, to judge by Lahore's Badshahi Masjid. Aurangzeb was far more similar to his Mughal predecessors than most people today recognize.

Aurangzeb also had marks of distinction, such as his prosaic concern with justice and his military acumen. Of course, earlier Mughal rulers were interested in providing justice, such as Jahangir, who claimed to have hung a large "chain of justice" with sixty bells from the Agra Fort to the riverbank that anybody could ring to get the king's attention. For Aurangzeb, justice was less showy and meant things such as cracking down on crooked administrators and guaranteeing safe religious festivals. Notwithstanding the emperor's intentions, however, Aurangzeb's administration was often notoriously bad on matters such as corruption. Moreover, while Aurangzeb demonstrated com-

mitment to his particular brand of ethics and morality throughout his life, he—like many other medieval kings—repeatedly
acted against his professed values to feed an insatiable hunger
for political power.

Aurangzeb was a brilliant military tactician at key moments,
perhaps the most outstanding general in the Mughal line. He
won the Peacock Throne by dominating a prolonged war of succession. And he took the Deccan, a prize sought after by the
Mughals for generations. Yet, somehow, an elderly Aurangzeb lost his way in southern India, aimlessly capturing forts
and growing increasingly toothless against administrators who
sought to take advantage of an aging king and weakened princes.

If Aurangzeb's reign had been twenty years shorter, closer
to that of Jahangir (who ruled for twenty-two years) or Shah
Jahan (who ruled for thirty years), modern historians would
judge him rather differently. But Aurangzeb's later decades of
fettering his sons, depending on an increasingly bloated administration, and undertaking ill-advised warring are a hefty part
of his tangled legacy. Thus, we are left with a mixed assessment
of a complex man and monarch who was plagued by an un-
bridgeable gap between his lofty ambitions and the realities of
Mughal India.

Unshackling Aurangzeb

I am what time, circumstance, history, have made of me, certainly, but I am,
also, much more than that. So are we all.

—*James Baldwin, American writer, 1955*

The Aurangzeb of popular memory bears only a faint resem-
blance to the historical emperor. This discrepancy is important
to recognize for two distinct reasons: defusing inflammatory
communal ideas and unshackling historical research.

In terms of Aurangzeb's popular reputation, India and Pakistan both suffer from politically fueled narratives of the Mughal past. As discussed, two visions of Aurangzeb feature in public discourse: Aurangzeb the Bigot and Aurangzeb the Pious. Especially misleading—and, at times, destructive—is the former image of Aurangzeb as a fanatic bent on destroying Hindus and Hinduism. Politicians and others in India deploy this notion in order to stir up anti-Muslim sentiment and brand Indian Muslims as dangerous traitors. Also problematic is labeling Aurangzeb an orthodox Muslim—"an Abraham in India's idol house," to quote the Persian and Urdu poet Muhammad Iqbal (d. 1938). This framing suggests that Muslims are primarily defined by their faith and that Islam is fundamentally at odds with Hinduism. For India, such ideas mean that Muslims cannot be fully Indian, whereas in Pakistan they suggest that all worthy citizens must adhere to a narrowly demarcated type of Islam.

.   .   .

A second reason why it is imperative to discard Aurangzeb's popular image is so that we can understand him in historical terms. Aurangzeb was a man of his times, not ours. I have argued that Aurangzeb acted according to his ideals of justice, commitment to political and ethical conduct (*adab* and *akhlaq*), and the necessities of politics. Aurangzeb's worldview was also shaped by his piety and the Mughal culture he inherited. He was not interested in fomenting Hindu-Muslim conflict— a modern obsession with modern stakes—but he was fixated on dispensing his brand of justice, upholding Mughal traditions, and expanding his grip across the subcontinent.

Aurangzeb nonetheless defies easy summarization. He was a man of studied contrasts and perplexing features. Aurangzeb was preoccupied with order—even fretting over the safety of the roads—but found no alternative to imprisoning his father, an action decried across much of Asia. He did not hesitate to slaughter family members, such as Dara Shukoh, or rip apart enemies, literally, as was the case with Sambhaji. He also sewed prayer caps by hand and professed a desire to lead a pious life. He was angered by bad administrators, rotten mangoes, and unworthy sons. He was a connoisseur of music and even fell in love with the musician Hirabai, but, beginning in midlife, deprived himself of appreciating the musical arts. Nonetheless, he passed his later years largely in the company of another musician, Udaipuri. He built the largest mosque in the world but chose to be buried in an unmarked grave. He died having expanded the Mughal kingdom to its greatest extent in history and yet feared utter failure.

Aurangzeb was an enigmatic king. Moreover, to quote Khafi Khan, the laudatory eighteenth-century historian of Aurangzeb's reign who compared the ruler to Jamshid, a legendary monarch in the Persian tradition, "To attempt a summary of the major events of a fifty-year reign of an emperor the equal of Jamshid is to measure the ocean's water with a pitcher." There remains much to say about this intriguing monarch and the kingdom that he ruled. Once we clear away the chaff of Aurangzeb the myth, we can confront the fascinating puzzle of Aurangzeb the king, a pivotal figure in the Indian medieval past.

A Note on Reading
Medieval Persian Texts

Aurangzeb's life and reign were documented in a vast array of sources. Histories, imperial orders, news reports, letters, travelogues, and other documents, written primarily in Persian, constitute an impressive amount of written material on this medieval Indian emperor. But historians struggle to make sound use of this abundant archive.

Historians lack access to many crucial documents and histories concerning Aurangzeb. Numerous sources never found their way into printed editions and so languish in manuscript libraries. Scholars require time and money to visit these libraries, which are scattered across South Asia and Europe, and many restrict photography such that it is near impossible to actually use their archival materials. Additionally, language training poses a challenge. The bulk of Mughal histories are written in Persian, the official administrative language of Aurangzeb's empire but a foreign tongue in India today. Out of necessity and ease, many historians disregard the original Persian texts and rely instead on English translations. This approach narrows the library of materials drastically, and many translations of Mughal texts are of questionable quality, brimming with mistranslations and abridgements. Some of these changes conveniently served the agendas of the translators, especially colonial-era translations that sought to show Indo-Muslim kings at their worst so that the British would seem virtuous by comparison (foremost here is Elliot and Dowson's *History of India, as Told by Its Own Historians*). Such materials are great resources for learning about British colonialism, but they present an inaccurate picture of Mughal India.

Even once scholars access and read documents from Aurangzeb's period, interpretation throws up substantial hurdles. Many of the so-called key historians of Aurangzeb's rule, such as Khafi Khan (*Muntakhab al-Lubab*) and Saqi Mustaid Khan (*Maasir-i Alamgiri*), wrote after Aurangzeb's death and relied extensively on memory and hearsay to reconstruct events that occurred decades earlier. Such a method allowed unintentional errors to creep into their chronicles, errors that can be sometimes detected by comparing these texts to eyewitness accounts, when available. Even documents that might seem more reliable, such as imperial orders and letters, often give a misleading depiction of events. Many orders were never carried out, for example.

In addition, many medieval writers did not obsess about getting the facts right. On the contrary, misrepresenting the past was a standard tactic among historians of Aurangzeb's day, who understood *tarikh* (the Persian genre of historical writing) as beholden to literary goals as much as accurately capturing the past. In addition to changing history to suit their literary needs, authors such as Khafi Khan employed heavy rhetoric that tells us a great deal about their own biases but obscures the causality behind specific imperial decisions. Such layered interests do not invalidate premodern historical narratives, but we must use such works with caution—appreciating both their literary and historical facets—in order to responsibly reconstruct Mughal history.

Most modern historians supplement Persian-medium Mughal chronicles with premodern works in other languages, including European travelogues, Hindi and other vernacular works, and (least commonly) Sanskrit texts. All of these bodies of materials throw up similar challenges in that they often mix fact and fiction. European travelogues deserve special mention because many scholars of the Mughal Empire have yet to grapple with how these works are not straightforward accounts of the facts but rather materials crafted with a particular audience (and, often, capitalist market) in mind.

Modern historians read historical sources with rigor. This means that we place texts in their wider social and literary contexts, weigh and assess evidence, and compare texts to one another. Historians also draw on material sources such as paintings, buildings, and coins. Ultimately historians use critical readings of primary sources to suggest a legitimate narrative arc that explains a historical figure, institution, or event. There is significant room for disagreement about history, and divergent interpretations are often constructive. But little is uncomplicated about the process of collecting, digesting, and making sense of historical sources on Aurangzeb.

Bibliographical Essay

This biography of Aurangzeb rests on the work of earlier scholars, both premodern and modern. In what follows I acknowledge that debt by detailing the works that I consulted, and I simultaneously provide an overview of some of the major sources for studying Aurangzeb. I have made limited use of manuscript archives, and most of my primary source research relies on printed editions. Readers interested in sources for quotes and other specific information should look at the Notes that follow this essay.

. . .

As I stated earlier, Persian histories form the backbone of our extensive historical resources on Aurangzeb Alamgir. Key events in Aurangzeb's early years are documented in Shah Jahan–period histories, including the following, which I draw from in this book: Abdul Hamid Lahawri's *Padshahnama*, Inayat Khan's *Shahjahannama*, Muhammad Salih Kambu's *Amal-i Salih*, and Tabatabai's *Shahjahannama*.

Several men penned histories during Aurangzeb's reign. Muhammad Kazim's *Alamgirnama*, ed. Khadim Husain and Abdul Hai (Calcutta, 1868), covers the first ten years of Aurangzeb's rule and is the only official court history. The *Mirat al-Alam* of Bakhtawar Khan (d. 1685) is a universal history that also covers the first decade of Aurangzeb's reign. As Sajida Alvi points out in *Perspectives on Mughal India* (Karachi, 2012), Bakhtawar Khan is little read today but sometimes provides additional information not found in the *Alamgirnama*. The *Waqiat-i Alamgiri* of Aqil Razi Khan (d. 1696/7) offers the most reliable account of the war of succession; I used Maulvi Zafar Hasan's edition (Delhi, 1946). There are additional unpublished Persian histories, such as Hatim Khan's *Alamgirnama*, Muhammad Masum's *Tarikh-i Shah Shujai*, and Abul Fazl Mamuri's *Tarikh-i Aurangzeb*, that I was unable to access in preparing this work.

Authors produced numerous histories in the few decades following Aurangzeb's death. Khafi Khan's *Muntakhab al-Lubab* (c. 1730)
and Saqi Mustaid Khan's *Maasir-i Alamgiri* (1710) are favorites among
many historians, partly because English translations are available,
translated by Moinul Haq (Karachi, 1975) and Jadunath Sarkar (Calcutta, 1947), respectively, and partly because they cover the entirety of
Aurangzeb's reign. Given their late dates and heavy use of rhetoric to
prop up an austere public image of Aurangzeb, I employ both with
caution and weigh them against other sources. I disregard Elliot and
Dowson's translation of Khafi Khan. Given its popularity, I cite Sarkar's
translation of the *Maasir-i Alamgiri*, but readers should be aware that
Sarkar's rendering is incomplete and contains errors (for more on this
translation see Tilmann Kulke, "A Mughal Munsi at Work" [European
University Institute, PhD diss., 2016], 10–15, 20–22).

Bhimsen Saxena's *Tarikh-i dilkusha* is an invaluable account of
events in the Deccan; I checked Sarkar's translation against a British
Library manuscript (Or. 23) and retranslated certain passages. Ishvardas, a Nagar Brahmin and Mughal civil officer in Jodhpur, wrote the
Futuhat-i Alamgiri, c. 1700 (Jadunath Sarkar incorrectly dated this text
to 1730). The *Futuhat* (Vadodara, 1995) contains some obvious historical inaccuracies but also offers compelling details not found in other
sources. The underutilized *Mirat-i Ahmadi* (1754) covers events in Gujarat during Aurangzeb's life. Shah Nawaz Khan's *Maasir al-Umara*,
ed. Abdur Rahim and Mirza Ashraf Ali (Calcutta, 1888–91), provides
short biographies of Mughal notables until 1780; also see the translation, *Maasir al-Umara*, trans. H. Beveridge and Baini Prashad (Patna,
1979).

In addition to Persian-language histories, I make limited use of
Hindi works, such as Bhushan's *Shivrajbhushan* (I thank Allison Busch
for the translation). I draw on Jain-authored vernacular works through
the scholarship of Jnan Chandra (on this topic also see Mohammad
Akram Lari Azad's *Religion and Politics in India* [Delhi, 1990], 234–37). I
delve briefly into Sikh materials via secondary sources. A more extensive
biography of Aurangzeb would take into account other Hindi works,
especially from Rajput courts, and perhaps even Sanskrit materials, such
as Lakshmipati's *Avadullacarita* and *Nripatinitigarbhitavritta*, that detail political events in the aftermath of Aurangzeb's death.

European travelogues are old standbys for historians of Aurangzeb's India, especially Niccoli Manucci's *Storia do Mogor*, trans. William Irvine (London, 1907–8), Francois Bernier's *Travels in the Mogul
Empire*, trans. Archibald Constable and Vincent Smith (Oxford, 1914),
and Jean-Baptiste Tavernier's *Voyages*, trans. V. Ball (London, 1889).
Here I also quote the less-popular accounts of Gemelli Careri, Peter
Mundy, William Norris, John Ovington, and Jean de Thevenot. Foreign travelers provide great insights into the Mughals, but scholars
have often privileged European works above Indian sources without
cause and failed to appreciate how Western travelers spun together
fantasy and reality.

. . .

I have allowed Aurangzeb to speak for himself a certain amount
through his letters, which often showcase a different persona than
Mughal histories that cover the same period. Aurangzeb penned many
Persian letters, and perhaps two thousand survive today. Several collections have been published, including *Adab-i Alamgiri, Kalimat-i
Taiyibat, Raqaim-i Karaim*, and *Ruqaat-i Alamgiri* (I largely use Bilimoria's English translation but adapt it to more closely represent the
original Persian). I have not used unpublished collections, such as
Dastur al-Amal Aghahi and *Ahkam-i Alamgiri* (the latter is not the
same text translated by Jadunath Sarkar as *Anecdotes of Aurangzeb*).
Sarkar's *Anecdotes* (Calcutta, 1917) is a tempting text with lots of juicy
tidbits about Aurangzeb, but it contains much misinformation (Sarkar
recognized this and details the veracity of some episodes in footnotes).
I draw on Sarkar's *Anecdotes* with caution and disregard entirely some
of the more likely fabrications included therein, such as Aurangzeb's
alleged second will (see *Anecdotes*, 51–55).

   Aurangzeb's words also come down to us in the more formal genre
of imperial orders (*farmans*) and their princely parallel, *nishans*. I especially rely on Jnan Chandra's articles on Aurangzeb's *farmans* concerning Hindu temples and religious communities and also on S. A. I.
Tirmizi's *Mughal Documents* (Delhi, 1995).

   News reports (*akhbarat*) of Aurangzeb's period survive in several
archives, although, owing to the limited scope of this book, I have only
accessed them through the reports of other scholars. For example, in
his *Princes of the Mughal Empire* (Cambridge, 2012), Munis Faruqui

made extensive use of the *Akhbarat-i darbar-i mualla* held in the National Library of India in Calcutta.

. . .

Secondary literature on Aurangzeb is vast but more shallow than one might like. Nineteenth-century biographies of Aurangzeb by Mountstuart Elphinstone (1841) and Stanley Lane-Poole (1893) remain in print but are outdated. I have not relied on such works here. Jadunath Sarkar (1870–1958), a self-made historian, made the most substantial contributions to scholarship on Aurangzeb in the twentieth century. He translated several Aurangzeb-period histories and a collection of letters into English and published numerous books on Aurangzeb, including the invaluable five-volume *History of Aurangzib* (1912–24). For a long while Sarkar had the last word on Aurangzeb. Relatively few scholars published on the king in the decades following Sarkar's exhaustive efforts. Scholars have slowly returned to studying Aurangzeb and have found him to be rather different from Sarkar's projection. While we all owe a debt to Jadunath Sarkar, his analysis was overly communal and sometimes lacked historical rigor. Those interested in thinking about Sarkar's methodology and legacy should consult Dipesh Chakrabarty's *The Calling of History: Sir Jadunath Sarkar and His Empire of Truth* (Chicago, 2015).

More recently, scholarship on Aurangzeb has expanded, and I draw on much of this work. In addition to the scholars I mention above, I have found the work of the following especially useful: M. Athar Ali, Satish Chandra, S. M. Azizuddin Husain, Irfan Habib, Harbans Mukhia, and John Richards. Many scholars have written on specific aspects of Aurangzeb's reign and inform my analysis here, including Catherine Asher (architecture), Richard M. Eaton (temple desecration), Louis Fenech (relations with Sikhs), Yohanan Friedmann (banning of Sirhindi), Jos Gommans (battles and Deccan years), Stewart Gordon (Mughal-Maratha conflict), B. N. Goswamy (Hindu ascetics), J. S. Grewal (Hindu ascetics and Sikhs), Alan Guenther (*Fatawa-i Alamgiri*), Robert Hallissey (relations with Rajputs), Shalin Jain (relations with Jains), Heidi Pauwels (Keshava Deva Temple), Katherine Butler Schofield (née Brown) (music), and Taymiya Zaman (Bhimsen Saxena). Vinay Lal's website, Manas (www.sscnet.ucla.edu/southasia/), offers short, accessible articles on the most controversial aspects of

Aurangzeb's reign. Several overviews of Mughal history show how Aurangzeb fit into the larger imperial Mughal project, including Michael H. Fisher, *A Short History of the Mughal Empire* (London, 2016); John F. Richards, *The Mughal Empire* (Cambridge, 1993); and Francis Robinson, *The Mughal Emperors and the Islamic Dynasties of India, Iran, and Central Asia, 1206–1925* (New York, 2007).

In writing this book, I had the privilege of drawing on unpublished and forthcoming work by several colleagues, including Supriya Gandhi (Dara Shukoh), Yael Rice (painting), and many of the contributors to the panels on Aurangzeb organized by Heidi Pauwels at the 2014 European Association for South-Asian Studies Conference, held in Zurich, Switzerland. Aurangzeb is a renewed topic of interest these days, and numerous scholars are poised to deepen the available secondary materials on him in the coming years.

.   .   .

Two final words are warranted on the wealth and paucity, respectively, of sources on Aurangzeb. Aurangzeb is already perhaps the most well-documented Mughal king, notwithstanding that many crucial sources, such as the *akhbarat*, are difficult for scholars to access. In addition, new material on Aurangzeb surfaces regularly. For example, a sword belonging to the emperor tumbled out of a cupboard at Aligarh Muslim University in 2011. Documentary materials also emerge on the private market, such as a *farman* issued by Aurangzeb that was sold by Christie's in 2014 for £27,500. Those looking to conduct serious research on Aurangzeb will suffer no lack of resources.

The casual reader and scholar alike, however, should be wary of what constitutes historical evidence and a legitimate historical claim. Individuals that claim to present "evidence" of Aurangzeb's supposed barbarism couched in the suspiciously modern terms of Hindu-Muslim conflict often trade in falsehoods, including fabricated documents and blatantly wrong translations. Many who condemn Aurangzeb have no training in the discipline of history and lack even basic skills in reading premodern Persian. Be skeptical of communal visions of Aurangzeb that flood the popular sphere. This biography aims to deepen our remarkably thin knowledge about the historical man and king, Aurangzeb Alamgir.

Notes

All translations are my own unless otherwise specified. For ease of reference, however, I have cited English translations where they are available.

Abbreviations

BL   British Library
IESHR   *Indian Economic and Social History Review*
IHR   *Indian Historical Review*
JAOS   *Journal of the American Oriental Society*
JAS   *Journal of Asian Studies*
JASB   *Journal of the Asiatic Society of Bengal*
JIP   *Journal of Indian Philosophy*
JPHS   *Journal of the Pakistan Historical Society*
JPS   *Journal of Persianate Studies*
MAS   *Modern Asian Studies*
SAHC   *South Asian History and Culture*

Chapter 1. Introducing Aurangzeb

UNFORGETTABLE AURANGZEB

"I came as a stranger": *Ruqaat-i Alamgiri* (Kanpur, 1870–90), 23 (my translation); see also *Ruqaat-i Alamgiri*, trans. Jamshid Bilimoria (Bombay, 1908), 71. **He expressed anxiety:** *Ruqaat-i Alamgiri*, Persian Kanpur ed., 24–25; see also *Ruqaat-i Alamgiri*, trans. Bilimoria, 73–74. **He admitted deeper doubts:** *Ruqaat-i Alamgiri*, Persian Kanpur ed., 23–24 (my translation); see also *Ruqaat-i Alamgiri*, trans. Bilimoria, 70–72. **150 million:** John Richards, *The Mughal Empire* (Cambridge, 1993), 1. **Aurangzeb's tomb:** *Maharashtra State Gazetteers* (Bombay, 1977), 4:1026–31.

THE MYTH OF AURANGZEB THE VILLAIN

"The last": Jawaharlal Nehru, *The Discovery of India* (Delhi, 1985), 265.
"tyrannical tormentor": Delhi Sikh Gurdwara Management Com-
mittee, petition on Change.org. **"Seeds of Partition were sown"**: Interview by *Tehelka*, May 9, 2015, http://www.tehelka.com/2015/05/seeds-of
-partition-were-sown-when-aurangzeb-triumphed-over-dara-shikoh/.
Nehru listed: Nehru, *Discovery of India*, 271, 265. **Alexander Dow:** *The
History of Hindostan* (London, 1772), available on Eighteenth Century
Collections Online, http://quod.lib.umich.edu/e/ecco/.

RECOVERING AURANGZEB THE MAN

"The stability of the foundation": *Ruqaat-i Alamgiri*, Persian Kan-
pur ed., 10; see also *Ruqaat-i Alamgiri*, trans. Bilimoria, 31. **akhlaq and
adab:** Muzaffar Alam, *The Languages of Political Islam* (Chicago, 2004);
Barbara Metcalf, ed., *Moral Conduct and Authority* (Berkeley, 1984).
Savarkar: Savarkar, *Hindutva*, cited in *Hindu Nationalism: A Reader*,
ed. Christophe Jaffrelot (Princeton, 2007), 92. **the word Hindu:** Carl
Ernst, *Eternal Garden* (Albany, 1992), 22–24; John Hawley, "Naming
Hinduism," *Wilson Quarterly* 15, no. 3 (1991): 22–24. **Mahabat Khan:**
Bhimsen, *Tarikh-i Dilkusha*, trans. Jadunath Sarkar (Bombay, 1972), 96;
and ms. BL Or. 23, fol. 59b.

Chapter 2. Early Years

THE INDIAN PRINCE'S CHILDHOOD

"It is hoped": *The Jahangirnama*, trans. Wheeler Thackston (New York,
1999), 282. **Aurangzeb was born:** Thackston, *The Jahangirnama*, 282, 284.
Using the Julian calendar, Aurangzeb's birthdate is sometimes given
as October 24, 1618; variation in Hijri-Gregorian conversion accounts
for it sometimes being listed as November 4. **Princely education:**
Munis Faruqui, *The Princes of the Mughal Empire* (Cambridge, 2012),
78–82; Munis Faruqui, "Awrangzib," Brill Online, 2015, http://reference
works.brillonline.com/entries/encyclopaedia-of-islam-3/awrangzib
-COM_23859. **fond of Rumi's Masnavi:** Sunil Sharma, "Performers in
Mughal Persian Texts," in *Tellings Not Texts*, ed. Francesca Orsini and
Katherine Schofield (Cambridge, 2015), 293–94. **Akbar recommended
the Mahabharata:** Audrey Truschke, *Culture of Encounters* (New York,
2016), 129. **compositions in Braj Bhasha:** Allison Busch, *Poetry of*

Kings (New York, 2011), 157. **Dara Shukoh's first wedding:** Milo Beach and Ebba Koch, *King of the World* (London, 1997); Peter Mundy, *The Travels of Peter Mundy in Europe and Asia, 1608–1667* (London, 1914), 2:202. **an elephant fight:** Supriya Gandhi, book in progress on Dara Shukoh; Aqil Khan Razi, *Waqiat-i Alamgiri*, ed. Zafar Hasan (Delhi, 1946); Abdul Hamid Lahawri, *Padshahnama*, trans. Wheeler Thackston in Beach and Koch, *King of the World*, 72–73 (see 74–75 on the surviving illustration of the event). **"Out of the gouge":** Tabatabai, *Shahjahan-nama*, ed. Syed Mohammad Yunus Jaffery (Delhi, 2009), 152. **a raging lion:** Beach and Koch, *King of the World*, 72–79. **Hirabai:** Katherine Brown, "Did Aurangzeb Ban Music?" *MAS* 41, no. 1 (2007): 82–85; Shah Nawaz Khan, *Maasir al-Umara*, trans. H. Beveridge and Baini Prashad (Patna, 1979), 1:806–7. **forced to withdraw:** Richards, *The Mughal Empire*, 157–58; Jagadish Sarkar, *The Life of Mir Jumla* (Calcutta, 1951), 123. **philosophical interests:** Rajeev Kinra, "Infantilizing Baba Dara," *JPS* 2 (2009): 165–93; Supriya Gandhi, "Mughal Engagements with Vedanta," in *Religious Interactions in Mughal India*, ed. Vasudha Dalmia and Munis Faruqui (Delhi, 2014), 65–101.

AURANGZEB SEIZED THE WORLD

"Ya takht ya tabut": Niccoli Manucci, *Storia do Mogor*, trans. William Irvine (London, 1907–8), 1:242; also given in slight variants elsewhere, such as *takht ast ya takhta* in Khafi Khan, *Muntakhab al-Lubab*, ed. Maulavi Kabir al-Din Ahmad (Calcutta, 1869), 2:596. **time-honored Mughal practices:** Faruqui, *Princes*. **European travelers were horrified:** Gemelli Careri, *Indian Travels*, ed. Surendranath Sen (Delhi, 1949), 230; John Ovington, *Voyage to Suratt* (London, 1696), 171–73; Francois Bernier, *Travels in the Mogul Empire*, trans. Archibald Constable and Vincent Smith (Oxford, 1914), 115. **death of Danyal:** Faruqui, *Princes*, 240–41. **overdosed on aphrodisiacs:** Manucci, *Storia*, 1:240. **"unruly passion":** Careri, *Indian Travels*, 222. **secret alliance:** Faruqui, *Princes*, 39. **"a wolf":** Aqil Khan Razi, *Waqiat-i Alamgiri*, 15 of Persian (my translation). **Dara's murderous intentions:** Aqil Khan Razi, *Waqiat-i Alamgiri*, 19 of English. **Three daughters chose:** Faruqui, *Princes*, 38. **Murad declared himself king:** Inayat Khan, *Shahjahan-nama*, ed. and trans. W. E. Begley and Z. A. Desai (Delhi, 1990), 545. **Aurangzeb vowed:** Faruqui, *Princes*, 40. **"Two hearts united":** Ishvardas, *Futuhat-i Alamgiri*, ed. Raghubir Sinh and Quazi Karamtullah,

trans. M. F. Lokhandwala and Jadunath Sarkar (Vadodara, 1995), 16
of English, 31 of Persian (my translation). **the punishing sun:** Aqil
Khan Razi, *Waqiat-i Alamgiri*, 20 of English. **"din of battle":** Khafi
Khan, *Muntakhab al-Lubab*, ed. Ahmad, 2:25; Khafi Khan, *History of Alamgir: Being an English translation of the relevant portions of
Muntakhab al-Lubab*, trans. Moinul Haq (Karachi, 1975), 26. **fire cannons and rockets:** Jadunath Sarkar, *History of Aurangzib* (Calcutta,
1912–24, repr. 2012), 2:57. **example of Joseph:** Aqil Khan Razi, *Waqiat-i
Alamgiri*, 25 of English. **last-ditch effort:** Sarkar, *History of Aurangzib*,
2:83–84. **pledged the prince:** Aqil Khan Razi, *Waqiat-i Alamgiri*, 23–24
of English; Inayat Khan, *Shahjahannama*, 552. **tensions surfaced:** Aqil
Khan Razi, *Waqiat-i Alamgiri*, 30–31 of English; cf. Ishvardas, *Futuhat-i
Alamgiri*, 30–33 of English. **lure his younger brother:** Aqil Khan Razi,
Waqiat-i Alamgiri, 32 of English. **Murad drank wine:** Manucci, *Storia*,
1:302. **a masseuse:** Ishvardas, *Futuhat-i Alamgiri*, 33 of English, 70–71 of
Persian; Manucci, *Storia*, 1:302. **twenty thousand men:** Aqil Khan Razi,
Waqiat-i Alamgiri, 33–34 of English.

KING OF HINDUSTAN

"When a celebration is adorned": Khafi Khan, *History of Alamgir*,
trans. Moinul Haq, 45; and *Muntakhab al-Lubab*, ed. Ahmad, 2:40 (my
translation). **the first of two coronation ceremonies:** Khafi Khan, *History of Alamgir*, trans. Moinul Haq, 44–45; and *Muntakhab al-Lubab*,
ed. Ahmad, 2:39–40; Aqil Khan Razi, *Waqiat-i Alamgiri*, 35 of English;
Inayat Khan, *Shahjahannama*, 553–54. **features noted by a later visitor:**
Careri, *Indian Travels*, 220. **led his dwindling troops:** Sarkar, *History
of Aurangzib*, 2:115–28, based largely on *Alamgirnama*. **Shah Shuja had
kept busy:** Sarkar, *History of Aurangzib*, 2:130, based on *Tarikh-i Shah
Shujai*. **battlegrounds glistened:** Ishvardas, *Futuhat-i Alamgiri*, 13 of
English, 25 of Persian. **Aurangzeb sent Shuja a letter:** Muhammad
Kazim, *Alamgirnama*, ed. Khadim Husain and Abdul Hai (Calcutta,
1868); Sarkar, *History of Aurangzib*, 2:137–38. **battlefield at Khajwa:** Aqil
Khan Razi, *Waqiat-i Alamgiri*, 37–40; Khafi Khan, *History of Alamgir*,
trans. Moinul Haq, 52–63. **met his death:** Rishad Choudhury, "Eventful Politics of Difference," *IESHR* 52, no. 3 (2015): 279–81; Stephan van
Galen, "Arakan and Bengal" (Leiden University, PhD diss., 2008),
chapter 7; Sarkar, *History of Aurangzib*, 2:286–88. **last major battle:**
Aqil Khan Razi, *Waqiat-i Alamgiri*, 43–45; Sarkar, *History of Aurangzib*,

2:171–84. **"Gunpowder smoke hung":** Muhammad Kazim, *Alamgir-nama*, 315 (my translation).

LIFE AND DEATH

"An emperor ought to stand": Jadunath Sarkar, *Anecdotes of Aurang-zib* (Calcutta, 1917), 58. **second coronation:** Khafi Khan, *Muntakhab al-Lubab*, ed. Ahmad, 2:76–78; and *History of Alamgir*, trans. Moinul Haq, 80–83 (merchants quote Haq's translation); Inayat Khan, *Shah-jahannama*, 558. **dressed in rags:** Muhammad Kazim, *Alamgirnama*, 414–19; Sarkar, *History of Aurangzib*, 2:211–12; Bernier, *Travels*, 98–99. **marched through Agra:** Khafi Khan, *History of Alamgir*, trans. Moinul Haq, 7. **Dara Shukoh was beheaded:** see, e.g., Ishvardas, *Futuhat-i Alamgiri*, 47 of English; Bhimsen, *Tarikh-i Dilkusha*, trans. Sarkar, 28 (omits apostasy); and Muhammad Kazim, *Alamgirnama*, 432, cited in Sarkar, *History of Aurangzib*, 2:214 (mentions apostasy). **Aurangzeb put Murad to death:** Khafi Khan, *History of Alamgir*, trans. Moinul Haq, 161; and *Muntakhab al-Lubab*, ed. Ahmad, 2:156. **overdosed on opium water:** Kambu, *Amal-i Salih*, cited in Sarkar, *History of Aurangzib*, 2:236. **Aurangzeb's body quartered:** Manucci, *Storia*, 1:357. **repaid the loans:** Shalin Jain, "Jains Under the Mughals," *IHR* 40 (2013): 86–87. **Zubdat-unnisa:** Saqi Mustaid Khan, *Maasir-i Alamgiri*, trans. Jadunath Sarkar (Calcutta, 1947), 77. **Prince Akbar:** Ibid., 73. **being irreverent:** Nathan Katz, "The Identity of a Mystic," *Numen* 47, no. 2 (2000): 142–60. **Aurangzeb executed Sarmad:** Kinra, "Infantilizing Baba Dara," 184–89. **Dara Shukoh's cross-cultural activities:** Truschke, *Culture of En-counters*, 234–38. **Aurangzeb dismissed him:** Rafat Bilgrami, "Shaykh 'Abd al-Wahhab," *JPHS* 31, no. 2 (1983): 101–2; S. M. Azizuddin Husain, *Structure of Politics Under Aurangzeb* (Delhi, 2002), 31. **sharif of Mecca:** Manucci, *Storia*, 2:114. **caustic letter:** Zafar Hasan, "Two Recently Discovered Letters," *Indian Historical Records Commission* (1920), 8–18. **eighty in all:** Khafi Khan, *History of Alamgir*, trans. Moinul Haq, 93–95; and *Muntakhab al-Lubab*, ed. Ahmad, 2:87–89.

Chapter 3: The Grand Arc of Aurangzeb's Reign

EXPANSION AND JUSTICE

"I wish you": Bernier, *Travels*, 168. **Mughal state revenues:** Lahawri, *Padshahnama*, cited in Richards, *The Mughal Empire*, 138–39. **"He was**

of a melancholy temperament": Manucci, *Storia*, 1:229. **Ishvaradasa:**
M. M. Patkar, "Muhurtaratna," *Poona Orientalist* 3 (1938): 82–85; Chris-
topher Minkowski, "Learned Brahmins and the Mughal Court," in
Dalmia and Faruqui eds., *Religious Interactions*, 119–21.

HEIR OF THE GRAND MUGHAL TRADITION

"In the region of Hindustan": *Ruqaat-i Alamgiri*, Persian Kanpur ed.,
26–27; *Ruqaat-i Alamgiri*, trans. Bilimoria, 81–82. **Bibi ka Maqbara:**
Catherine Asher, *Architecture of Mughal India* (Cambridge, 1992), 263–
64. **The king appeared daily:** Khafi Khan, *History of Alamgir*, trans.
Moinul Haq, 215–16; Saqi Mustaid Khan, *Maasir-i Alamgiri*, 213; Ber-
nier, *Travels*. **publicly weighed:** Khafi Khan, *History of Alamgir*, trans.
Moinul Haq; Saqi Mustaid Khan, *Maasir-i Alamgiri*; Bernier, *Travels*.
Anand Nath: B. N. Goswamy and J. S. Grewal, *The Mughals and the
Jogis of Jakhbar* (Simla, 1967), 120–24, 32–33. **art of music:** Bakhtawar
Khan, *Mirat al-Alam*, ed. Sajida Alvi (Lahore, 1979), 1:385; and translated
in Sajida Alvi, *Perspectives on Mughal India* (Karachi, 2012), 65; Brown,
"Did Aurangzeb Ban Music?" **reassigned the author:** Husain, *Structure
of Politics*, 155–67. **enhanced salaries:** *Alamgirnama*, 448, cited in Bonnie
Wade, *Imaging Sound* (Chicago, 1998), 187. **recommended the weighing
rites:** *Ruqaat-i Alamgiri*, Persian Kanpur ed., 25–26; and *Ruqaat-i Alamgiri*, trans. Bilimoria, 78–79. **the 1690 report:** Ovington, *Voyage to Suratt*,
178–79. **penname Makhfi:** Part of Zebunnisa's alleged diwan was translated by Magan Lal and Jessie Westbrook, *The Diwan of Zeb-un-Nissa*
(New York, 1913). **Kavindracarya found employment:** P. K. Gode,
Studies in Indian Literary History (Bombay, 1954), 2:364–79; P. K. Gode,
Studies in Indian Cultural History (Poona, 1969), 3:71–79. **a noted patron
of Sanskrit:** Truschke, *Culture of Encounters*, 236–37. **Gujarishatakam:**
Siddharth Wakankar, *Literary Gems from Sanskrit Literature* (Delhi,
2002), 65–80. **Fatawa-i Alamgiri:** Alan Guenther, "Hanafi fiqh in Mu-
ghal India," in *India's Islamic Traditions*, ed. Richard M. Eaton (New
Delhi, 2003), 209–30; Mouez Khalfaoui, "al-Fatawa l-'Alamgiriyya,"
Brill Online, 2015, http://dx.doi.org/10.1163/1573-3912_ei3_COM_27028.
spent one million rupees: *Kalimat-i Taiyibat*, cited in Husain, *Structure
of Politics*, 108, 126n107. **Badshahi Masjid:** Asher, *Architecture of Mughal
India*, 257–60; William Glover, *Making Lahore Modern* (Minneapolis,
2008), 19. **wrote out answers:** Careri, *Indian Travels*, 220–21. **"King [Au-
rangzeb] undertakes":** Ibid., 247. **a court astrologer recommended:**

Khafi Khan, *History of Alamgir*, trans. Moinul Haq, 539. **Chandraman dedicated his Nargisistan:** *Nargisistan*, Nawal Kishore lithographed edition (1875); *Nargisistan*, ed. Muhammad Kazim Kahduyi (Qom, 2013). **Amar Singh followed suit:** *Ramayan: Kitab-i Muqaddas-i Hinduan*, ed. Abdul Wudud Azhar Dihlavi (Tehran, 1971) (dedication and date, 3). **Persian Ramayanas:** Fathullah Mujtabai, *Aspects of Hindu Muslim Cultural Relations* (Delhi, 1978), 68–71; N. S. Shukla, "Persian Translations of Sanskrit Works," *Indological Studies* 3, no. 1–2 (1974): 183–84.

Chapter 4: Administrator of Hindustan

WATCHING OVER HIS VAST EMPIRE

"Shah Jahan used to hold": Bhimsen, *Tarikh-i Dilkusha*, trans. Sarkar, 255; ms. BL Or. 23, fol. 157a (adapted from Sarkar's translation). **Herbert de Jager:** Jos Gommans, *Mughal Warfare* (London, 2002), 94. **Careri complained:** Careri, *Indian Travels*, 216; *Ruqaat-i Alamgiri*, Persian Kanpur ed., 9; and *Ruqaat-i Alamgiri*, trans. Bilimoria, 26–27. **accepted bribes:** Bhimsen, *Tarikh-i Dilkusha*, trans. Sarkar, 142–43. **"had a long arm":** Shah Nawaz Khan, *Maasir al-Umara*, trans. Beveridge and Prashad, 1:75. **"sovereignty does not stand":** *Ruqaat-i Alamgiri*, Persian Kanpur ed., 40 (my translation); and *Ruqaat-i Alamgiri*, trans. Bilimoria, 130–31. **Shivaji did not forget:** Bhimsen, *Tarikh-i Dilkusha*; Ishvardas, *Futuhat-i Alamgiri*; Khafi Khan, *Muntakhab al-Lubab*; Thevenot, *Indian Travels*, ed. Sen (Delhi, 1949); Bakhtawar Khan, *Mirat al-Alam*. **"If it had been":** Sarkar, *Anecdotes*, 72–73. **Akbar declared himself emperor:** Robert Hallissey, *The Rajput Rebellion* (Columbia, 1977), 67–74; Faruqui, *Princes*, 206–7. **Sambhaji received no mercy:** Bhimsen, *Tarikh-i Dilkusha*, trans. Sarkar, 169; Khafi Khan, *History of Alamgir*, trans. Moinul Haq, 386–88; and *Muntakhab al-Lubab*, ed. Ahmad, 2:387–89; Ishvardas, *Futuhat-i Alamgiri*, 160 of English; Manucci, *Storia*, 2:311–12. **executed Tegh Bahadur:** Satish Chandra, "Guru Tegh Bahadur's Martyrdom," *The Hindu* (Oct. 16, 2001); Louis Fenech, *The Sikh Zafar-namah* (New York, 2013), 107–9; J. S. Grewal, *Guru Tegh Bahadur and the Persian Chroniclers* (Amritsar, 1976); J. S. Grewal and Irfan Habib, eds., *Sikh History from Persian Sources* (New Delhi, 2001). **location of Tegh Bahadur's execution:** Grewal, *Guru Tegh Bahadur*, 80–81. **Kashmiri Brahmins:** Louis Fenech, "Martyrdom and the Sikh Tradition," *JAOS* 117, no. 4 (1997): 623–35; Hardip Singh Syan, *Sikh*

Militancy in the Seventeenth Century (London, 2012), 130–35. **supported Dara Shukoh:** J. S. Grewal, *The Sikhs of the Punjab* (Cambridge, 1990), 69. **Satnamis:** Khafi Khan, *History of Alamgir*, trans. Moinul Haq, 255–57; and *Muntakhab al-Lubab*, ed. Ahmad, 2:252–54.

PRIZED HINDU NOBLES

"O King": Quoted in Rajeev Kinra, *Writing Self, Writing Empire* (Oakland, 2015), 54 (Kinra's translation). **split in their support:** M. Athar Ali, *The Mughal Nobility Under Aurangzeb* (Delhi, 1997), 96; M. Athar Ali, *Mughal India* (Delhi, 2006), 249–50. **Chandar Bhan Brahman:** Kinra, *Writing Self*, 54–57, 82–83. **Hindu share in Mughal administration:** Ali, *Mughal Nobility*, 31. **pledged loyalty:** Aqil Khan Razi, *Waqiat-i Alamgiri*, 24 of English. **Aurangzeb appointed Raghunatha:** Shah Nawaz Khan, *Maasir al-Umara*, ed. Abdur Rahim and Mirza Ashraf Ali (Calcutta, 1890), 2:282; and *Maasir al-Umara*, trans. Beveridge and Prashad, 2:559–60; Ali, *Mughal India*, 250–51; Bhimsen, *Tarikh-i Dilkusha*, trans. Sarkar, 28; Khafi Khan, *History of Alamgir*, trans. Moinul Haq, 82. **acting vizier:** Bernier, *Travels*, 391. **"frontispiece in the book":** Kinra, *Writing Self*, 53 (Kinra's translation). **Raghunatha's life was cut short:** Khafi Khan, *History of Alamgir*, trans. Moinul Haq, 179. **"the work of government":** *Ruqaat-i Alamgiri*, Persian Kanpur ed., 20–21, 44; and *Ruqaat-i Alamgiri*, trans. Bilimoria, 60, 142–43 (my translation). **"it was a practice":** Bhimsen, *Tarikh-i Dilkusha*, trans. Sarkar, 83; ms. BL Or. 23, fol. 50b (Sarkar's translation). **Muslim from Bukhara:** Sarkar, *Anecdotes*, 97–100 (Sarkar's translation).

MARATHA AND RAJPUT RESISTANCE

"A governorship from Delhi": Bhushan Tripathi, *Shivrajbhushan* (Delhi, 1982), v. 163, translated by Allison Busch, "'Unhitching the Oxcart of Delhi': Mughal-Period Hindi Accounts of Political Insurgency," *Journal of the Royal Asiatic Society* (forthcoming). **Brahmin-led ritual:** Stewart Gordon, *The Marathas* (Cambridge, 1993), 87–88. **destructive assaults:** Gordon, *The Marathas*, 59–80; Richards, *The Mughal Empire*, 205–16; Gommans, *Mughal Warfare*, 60–61. **Shivaji visited Aurangzeb's court:** Bhimsen, *Tarikh-i Dilkusha*, trans. Sarkar, 48–51 ("madman"); Thevenot, *Indian Travels*, 41–43; Khafi Khan, *History of Alamgir*, trans. Moinul Haq, 192–94, 201–4; and *Muntakhab al-Lubab*, ed. Ahmad, 2:189–91, 2:198–201 ("wounded animal"; escaped in baskets). **dressed as**

a Brahmin's wife: Bhimsen, *Tarikh-i Dilkusha*, trans. Sarkar, 51. **raided Mughal strongholds:** Gordon, *The Marathas*, 79–80; Richards, *The Mughal Empire*, 212. **putting down Pathan tribal revolts:** Richards, *The Mughal Empire*, 170–71. **Shivaji crowned himself:** V. S. Bendrey, *Coronation of Shivaji* (Bombay, 1960). **Rajavyavaharakosha:** Audrey Truschke, "Defining the Other," *JIP* 40, no. 6 (2012): 660; Sumit Guha, "Bad Language and Good Language," in *Forms of Knowledge in Early Modern Asia*, ed. Sheldon Pollock (Durham, 2011), 60–62. **poisoned her husband:** Jadunath Sarkar, *Shivaji and His Times* (London, 1920), 383. **brief succession struggle:** Gordon, *The Marathas*, 91. **Aurangzeb as Kumbhakarna:** Aziz Ahmad, "Epic and Counter-Epic," *JAOS* 83, no. 4 (1963): 476. **called Shivaji a "mountain rat":** Gordon, *The Marathas*, 84. **brusque chronogram:** Abhishek Kaicker, "Unquiet City" (Columbia University, PhD diss., 2014), 313. **Shivaji allied:** Gordon, *The Marathas*, 81. **Shivaji welcomed Muslims:** Gordon, *The Marathas*, 66. **Rathor-Sisodia rebellion:** Hallissey, *The Rajput Rebellion*; Richards, *The Mughal Empire*, 179–84; G. D. Sharma, *Rajput Polity* (Delhi, 1977), 160–94.

Chapter 5: Moral Man and Leader

PIETY AND POWER

"The Emperor [Aurangzeb] wrote": Bhimsen, *Tarikh-i Dilkusha*, trans. Sarkar, 215. **Aurangzeb memorized:** Saqi Mustaid Khan, *Maasir-i Alamgiri*, trans. Sarkar, 317–18. **sewed prayer caps:** Careri, *Indian Travels*, 237. **copied the Quran:** Saqi Mustaid Khan, *Maasir-i Alamgiri*, trans. Sarkar, 317–18. **Shiv Mangaldas Maharaj:** Faruqui, "Awrangzib"; Satish Chandra, *Mughal Religious Policies* (Delhi, 1993), 207. **depicts his visit:** Amherst College image; Yael Rice's description of image at http://museums.fivecolleges.edu/; Khafi Khan, *History of Alamgir*, trans. Moinul Haq, 257–58. **wrote out prayers:** Khafi Khan, *History of Alamgir*, trans. Moinul Haq, 257; and *Muntakhab al-Lubab*, ed. Ahmad, 2:254. **Aurangzeb dismounted:** Saqi Mustaid Khan, *Maasir-i Alamgiri*, trans. Sarkar, 317. **"You should consider":** *Kalimat-i Taiyibat*, quoted in translation in Chandra, *Mughal Religious Policies*, 205–6. **Aurangzeb's "rigorous abstinence":** Careri, *Indian Travels*, 231. **delegation of Bijapuri theologians:** *Basatin-i Salatin*, quoted in Sarkar, *History of Aurangzib*, 4:386. **Bijapuri palace wall paintings:** Sarkar, *History of Aurangzib*, 4:391. **"decide the case":** Sarkar, *Anecdotes*, 141–42. **Shaykh**

al-Islam: Khafi Khan, *History of Alamgir*, trans. Moinul Haq, 345; and *Muntakhab al-Lubab*, ed. Ahmad, 2:343. **collectors of the jizya tax:** Chandra, *Mughal Religious Policies*, 170–89; Irfan Habib, *The Agrarian System* (Delhi, 1999), 285–87. **jizya tax had been abated:** K. A. Nizami, *Akbar and Religion* (Delhi, 1989), 107–8, cited in Richards, *The Mughal Empire*, 39. **lampooned the jizya:** Ali, *Mughal India*, 207 (based on the *akhbarat* and Manucci). **scathing letter:** translated in Sarkar, *History of Aurangzib*, 3:325–29; on its authorship see Hallissey, *The Rajput Rebellion*, 87–88. **greedy tax collectors:** Bhimsen, *Tarikh-i Dilkusha*, trans. Sarkar, 231; Manucci, *Storia*, 2:415.

MORAL POLICING

"A king is a shepherd": Sa'di, *Gulistan*, trans. Wheeler Thackston (Bethesda, 2008), 37–38. **Shanticandra wrote:** *Kriparasakosha*, ed. Jinavijaya (Bhavnagar, 1917), v. 102 (my translation). **Jahangir also claimed:** Thackston, *The Jahangirnama*, 26. **"prohibited equally":** Bernier, *Travels*, 252–53. **"fond of nothing more":** Harihar Das, *The Norris Embassy to Aurangzib* (Calcutta, 1959), 268, 274 (I have modernized the English spellings). **"But with respect":** Manucci, *Storia*, 2:5–6. **opium:** Habib, *Agrarian System*, 49–50. **Aurangzeb constrained:** Bhimsen, *Tarikh-i Dilkusha*, trans. Sarkar, 51. **Armed bands of ascetics:** Ibid., 32. **Muharram celebrations:** Khafi Khan, *History of Alamgir*, trans. Moinul Haq, 216–17; and *Muntakhab al-Lubab*, ed. Ahmad, 2:213–14; Thevenot, *Indian Travels*, 148–50. **Aurangzeb ordered his officials:** *Kalimat-i Taiyibat*, ed. S. M. Azizuddin Husain (Delhi, 2009), no. 8; Ali Muhammad Khan, *Mirat-i Ahmadi*, trans. M. F. Lokhandwala (Baroda, 1965), 233. **rescinding taxes:** Khafi Khan, *History of Alamgir*, trans. Moinul Haq, 93–95; and *Muntakhab al-Lubab*, ed. Ahmad, 2:87–89. **Holi celebrations:** Careri, *Indian Travels*, 210, 363n21; Thevenot, *Indian Travels*, 81; Bhimsen, *Tarikh-i Dilkusha*, trans. Sarkar, 95. **Aurangzeb chastised:** *Ruqaat-i Alamgiri*, Persian Kanpur ed., 3; and *Ruqaat-i Alamgiri*, trans. Bilimoria, 5–6. **1699 letter:** Chandra, *Mughal Religious Policies*, 202. **few Hindus converted:** Faruqui, "Awrangzib"; also see list of Hindu converts from *Maasir-i Alamgiri*, in Zahiruddin Faruki, *Aurangzeb and His Times* (Bombay, 1935), 180–81. **Ahmad Sirhindi:** Yohanan Friedmann, "Naqshbandis and Awrangzeb," in *Naqshbandis*, ed. Marc Gaborieau, Alexandre Popovic, and Thierry Zarcone (Istanbul, 1990), 209–20; Faruqui, "Awrangzib." **Mahdavis:** Samira Sheikh, "Aurangzeb as Seen from Gujarat: Shi'i and Millenarian Challenges to Mughal Sovereignty" (in preparation); Derryl Maclean, "Mahdawiyah and the State," in Eaton ed., *India's Islamic Traditions*, 160–63. **Ismaili Bohras:** Sheikh, "Aurangzeb as Seen from Gujarat." **banned music:** Brown, "Did Aurangzeb Ban Music?" **satirical poetry:** Sarkar, *Anecdotes*, 127–28 (brackets in the original); the opening line of the satire of Kamgar Khan is cited in Shah Nawaz Khan, *Maasir al-Umara*, trans. Beveridge and Prashad, 1:761.

Chapter 6: Overseer of Hindu Religious Communities

PROTECTOR OF TEMPLES

"[Ellora] is one": *Kalimat-i Taiyibat*, 13 (my translation); also translated in Faruqui, "Awrangzib." **counted Hindus:** Yohanan Friedmann, *Tolerance and Coercion in Islam* (Cambridge, 2003), 84–85. **"Because the persons":** Ali, *Mughal India*, 246; Shyamaldas, *Viravinoda: Mewar ka itihas* (Delhi, 1986), 2:419–20n (my translation adapted from Ali's). **"several people have":** Richard M. Eaton, "Temple Desecration and Indo-Muslim States," *Frontline*, Jan. 5, 2001, 71 (Eaton's translation); D. C. Phillott, "Firman of Emperor Aurangzeb," *JASB* 7 (1911): 689–90. **farman to the Umanand Temple:** Jnan Chandra, "Aurangzib and Hindu Temples," *JPHS* 5, no. 1 (1957): 251. **Bhagwant Gosain:** Ibid., 248–49. **Ramjivan Gosain:** Ibid., 250 (quote is Chandra's translation). **conferred eight villages:** Jalaluddin, "Some Important Farmans and Sanads," *Studies in Islam* 15–16 (1978): 40–48. **Rang Bhatt:** Jnan Chandra, "'Alamgir's Grant to a Brahmin," *JPHS* 7, no. 2 (1959): 99–100. **Jangam:** Jnan Chandra, "Alamgir's Patronage of Hindu Temples," *JPHS* 6, no. 1 (1958): 208–13; Jnan Chandra, "Aurangzib and Hindu Temples," 249–50; M. A. Ansari, *Administrative Documents of Mughal India* (Delhi, 1984), docs. 1–20. **favorable policies toward Jain religious institutions:** Jain, "Jains Under the Mughals," 88–89; Chandra, "Aurangzib and Hindu Temples," 252–53; Jnan Chandra, "Alamgir's Tolerance in the Light of Contemporary Jain Literature," *JPHS* 6, no. 1 (1958): 269–72; Jnan Chandra, "Alamgir's Attitude Towards Non-Muslim Institutions," *JPHS* 7, no. 1 (1959): 36–39. **"mardano aur mahabali":** Chandra, "Alamgir's Tolerance," 272 (my translation). **recalling all endowed lands:** Habib, *Agrarian System*, 356–57. **gave more endowed land to Hindus:** Richard M. Eaton, *The Rise of Islam and the Bengal Frontier, 1204–1760* (Berkeley, 1993), 263. **Parsi**

physicians received confirmation: Habib, *Agrarian System*, 357n67. **"on paper only":** M. L. Bhatia, *The Ulama, Islamic Ethics and Courts* (Delhi, 2006), 46–47. **"ancient temples should not":** Eaton, "Temple desecration and Indo-Muslim States," 72–74 (Eaton's translation).

DESTROYER OF TEMPLES

"It is not lawful": Quoted by Nizamuddin Ahmad in his *Tabaqat-i Akbari*, trans. B. De, cited in Eaton, "Temple Desecration and Indo-Muslim States," 70. **Richard Eaton:** "Temple Desecration in Pre-modern India," *Frontline*, Dec. 22, 2000; "Temple Desecration and Indo-Muslim States"; Richard M. Eaton, interview by Ajaz Ashraf, *Scroll.in* (Nov. 20, 2015), http://scroll.in/article/769463/we-will-never-know-the-number-of-temples-desecrated-through-indias-history-richard-eaton. **two orders:** Romila Thapar, *Somanatha* (Delhi, 2004), 68; Sheikh, "Aurangzeb as Seen from Gujarat." **he ordered mihrabs:** S. A. I. Tirmizi, *Mughal Documents* (Delhi, 1995), 2:11, 89; cf. Ali Muhammad Khan, *Mirat-i Ahmadi*, trans. Lokhandwala, 194. **"a rare and impossible event":** Saqi Mustaid Khan, *Maasir-i Alamgiri*, ed. Maulawi Agha Ahmad Ali (Calcutta, 1871), 96 (my translation); and Saqi Mustaid Khan, *Maasir-i Alamgiri*, trans. Sarkar, 60. **Vishvanatha Temple:** Surendra Sinha, *Subah of Allahabad* (Delhi, 1974), 65–68; Rosalind O'Hanlon, "Letters Home," *MAS* 44, no. 2 (2010): 234–35; Asher, *Architecture of Mughal India*, 278. **Keshava Deva Temple:** Asher, *Architecture of Mughal India*, 254, 259–60; Heidi Pauwels, "Tale of Two Temples," *SAHC* 2, no. 2 (2011): 288–90; Sri Ram Sharma, *The Religious Policy of the Mughal Emperors* (Delhi, 1988), 63. **"If a Shiva linga":** Quoted in translation in Richard Davis, *Lives of Indian Images* (Princeton, 1999), 53. **Hindu kings targeted one another's temples:** Davis, *Lives of Indian Images*, 51–85; Eaton, "Temple Desecration in Pre-modern India," 65–66; Michael Willis, *Temples of Gopaksetra* (London, 1997), 96. **Gyanvapi Masjid:** Asher, *Architecture of Mughal India*, 277–79. **degeneracy of the Kali Yuga:** Phyllis Granoff, "Responses to Muslim Iconoclasm," *East and West* 41 (1991): 189–203. **"deviant Brahmins were teaching":** Saqi Mustaid Khan, *Maasir-i Alamgiri*, ed. Ali, 81 (my translation); Eaton, "Temple Desecration and Indo-Muslim States," 74; cf. mistranslation in Saqi Mustaid Khan, *Maasir-i Alamgiri*, trans. Sarkar, 51–52. **Akbar took Brahmins to task:** Truschke, *Culture of Encounters*, 131–32. **"find their Profit":** Thevenot, *Indian Travels*, 96.

Chapter 7: Later Years

CONQUEROR OF THE DECCAN

"I have found": Bhimsen, *Tarikh-i Dilkusha*, trans. Sarkar, 223; ms. BL Or. 23, fol. 134a (adapted from Sarkar's translation). **"If a man of God":** Sa'di, *Gulistan*, trans. Thackston, 15. **moved to the Deccan:** Khafi Khan, *History of Alamgir*, trans. Moinul Haq, 282–83; Richards, *The Mughal Empire*, 219. **ghost town:** Stephen Blake, *Shahjahanabad: The Sovereign City in Mughal India* (Cambridge, 1991), 67–68. **besieged Bijapur:** Richards, *The Mughal Empire*, 220–21; Sarkar, *History of Aurangzib*, 4:374–94. **Golconda:** John Richards, *Mughal Administration in Golconda* (Oxford, 1975), 46–51; Richards, *The Mughal Empire*, 221–22. **more than one-quarter:** Richards, *The Mughal Empire*, 223. **"They are dark":** Bhimsen, *Tarikh-i Dilkusha*, trans. Sarkar, 194. **jagirs:** Ali, *Mughal Nobility*, 92–94; Satish Chandra, *Parties and Politics* (Delhi, 2002), 29–39. **siege of Jinji:** Gommans, *Mughal Warfare*, 187–97; Gordon, *The Marathas*, 95–97. **"no release from labour":** Sarkar, *Anecdotes*, 107. **Deccan's fresh air:** *Adab-i Alamgiri*, quoted in Sarkar, *History of Aurangzib*, 1:235–36. **Bijapur's population:** Richard M. Eaton, *Sufis of Bijapur, 1300–1700* (Princeton, 1978), 270. **remitting the jizya:** Chandra, *Mughal Religious Policies*, 182, 189n61.

DYING KING

"Too great is the grief": Quoted in Annemarie Schimmel, *A Two-Colored Brocade* (Chapel Hill, 1992), 295 (Schimmel's translation). **"When the mango is good":** *The Baburnama*, trans. Wheeler Thackston (Washington, 1996), 344 (italics mine). **send baskets of mangoes:** *Ruqaat-i Alamgiri*, trans. Bilimoria, 60, 100. **named unfamiliar species:** *Ruqaat-i Alamgiri*, Persian Kanpur ed., 5; and *Ruqaat-i Alamgiri*, trans. Bilimoria, 12. **"Babaji, dhun, dhun":** *Ruqaat-i Alamgiri*, Persian Kanpur ed., 15; and *Ruqaat-i Alamgiri*, trans. Bilimoria, 46. **Udaipuri:** Brown, "Did Aurangzeb Ban Music?" 98. **a deathbed letter to Kam Bakhsh:** *Ruqaat-i Alamgiri*, Persian Kanpur ed., 24; and *Ruqaat-i Alamgiri*, trans. Bilimoria, 74. **"A daughter is better":** *Ruqaat-i Alamgiri*, Persian Kanpur ed., 3; and *Ruqaat-i Alamgiri*, trans. Bilimoria, 4 (my translation adapted from Bilimoria). **arrested Kam Bakhsh:** Faruqui, *Mughal Princes*, 298–99. **Aurangzeb's purported last will:** translated in Sarkar, *History of Aurangzib*, 5:212–13, from an undated manuscript of documents collected in 1743 (BL India Office no. 1344); also see the second alleged final will of

Aurangzeb translated in Sarkar, *History of Aurangzib*, 5:213–16. **Aurang-
zeb proffered advice:** *Ruqaat-i Alamgiri*, Persian Kanpur ed., 25–26; and
Ruqaat-i Alamgiri, trans. Bilimoria, 78–89 (my translation adapted from
Bilimoria). **report by the chaplain John Ovington:** Ovington, *Voyage to
Suratt*, 178–79. **endorsed Shah Jahan's enjoyment of music:** *Ruqaat-i
Alamgiri*, Persian Kanpur ed., 5–7; and *Ruqaat-i Alamgiri*, trans. Bilimo-
ria, 14–19. **he was interred:** Ernst, *Eternal Garden*, 223–25.

Chapter 8: Aurangzeb's Legacy

AFTER AURANGZEB

"None but the Creator": Simon Digby, trans., *Sufis and Soldiers in
Awrangzeb's Deccan: Malfuzat-i Naqshbandiyya* (Delhi, 2001), 143.
Mughal kingdom after Aurangzeb's death: Faruqui, *Princes*, 309–23;
Michael Fisher, *A Short History of the Mughal Empire* (London, 2016),
209–12; Richards, *The Mughal Empire*, 253–81; Chandra, *Parties and
Politics*; Muzaffar Alam, *The Crisis of Empire in Mughal North India*
(Delhi, 1986). **Nadir Shah sacked Delhi:** Chandra, *Parties and Politics*,
283–92; Fisher, *A Short History*, 216–17; Kaicker, "Unquiet City," 475–577.
portrait of Nadir Shah: Victoria and Albert Museum, IM.20-1919. **"a
child's game":** Quoted in translation in Ayesha Jalal, *Partisans of Allah*
(Cambridge, 2008), 53. **East India Company stripped:** Fisher, *A Short
History*, 219–24. **Akbar Shah II:** Emma Roberts, *Scenes and Character-
istics of Hindostan* (London, 1835), 3:179–82. **the fall of Mughal power:**
Richards, Pearson, and Hardy contributions to "Symposium: Decline
of the Mughal Empire," *JAS* 35, no. 2 (1976); Meena Bhargava, ed., *The
Decline of the Mughal Empire* (Delhi, 2014). **"the Mughal crescent":**
Sarkar, *History of Aurangzib*, 1:xiii. **"The life of Aurangzib":** Sarkar, *History of Aurangzib*, 5:1. **"chain of justice":** Thackston, *The Jahangirnama*,
24.

UNSHACKLING AURANGZEB

"I am what time": *Notes of a Native Son* (1955). **"Abraham in India's
idol house":** Muhammad Iqbal, "Emperor Alamgir and the Tiger,"
in *Rumuz-i Bekhudi*, trans. Arberry, www.allamaiqbal.com; original Persian in Faruki, *Aurangzeb*, 562n24. **"To attempt a summary":**
Khafi Khan, *History of Alamgir*, trans. Moinul Haq, 3; and *Muntakhab
al-Lubab*, ed. Ahmad, 2:2 (my translation).

Index

Lightning Source UK Ltd.
Milton Keynes UK
UKHW010702120122
397010UK00006B/265